RAILWAYS of WEMBLEY

FRANK GOUDIE

Robert Barker   Douglas Stuckey

When melancholy Autumn comes to Wembley
And electric trains are lighted after tea
The poplars near the Stad
With their tap and tap a
Like the sound of little br
Spreading out along the s
When the estuary's filling

C000161659

Contents

© 1996

FORGE BOOKS

55 Brookside,
Wokingham
Berks

The London and Birmingham Railway, 1835. The bridge at Kenton Road long before it acquired a station.

Mk3 DVT No 82103 hares through Wembley Central on 11 April 1992, heading the 14.48 Birmingham New Street-Euston train. Class 90 No 9007 "Lord Stamp" is providing power from the rear.

BRIAN MORRISON

Foreword by Ken Livingstone M.P.

This enjoyable and entertaining account of the railways of Wembley appears when the debate over the future of our public transport is at its most furious. Transport in Wembley is no purely local concern; it has to provide carriage on an irregular basis for millions moving to and from the events – cup finals, concerts and religious revivals – which make Wembley famous. Whatever happens elsewhere it seems that in Wembley a good and co-ordinated provision of train, bus and tube services will be of national importance in the years to come.

The fragmentation of British Rail is regarded with apprehension by a broad spectrum of people irrespective of their normal political allegiances. London's government has gone and London Transport as we knew it is going but, given Lord Howe's recent confession that abolishing the GLC was a mistake, we may shortly see London government reappear in a new form. Clearly its single most important function would be transport. Within Wembley, at places like Sudbury Town station, we can still see reminders (albeit a little faded) of the time in the 1930's when London Transport harnessed art and science to give Londoners a transport system which they could use with pleasure and talk of with pride.

This is no place for a long polemic – not all imaginative developments in public transport happened under one political party only – but our local history may suggest lessons from the past to help in planning an environmentally-friendly transport system for the future. London and its environs need a renaissance, not only to charge their economy and make their visitors welcome, but to give thier citizens a proper joy in living in the greatest of cities. in such a renaissance public transport will be crucial.

Ken Livingstone

STATIONS: Alperton, thence bus 83 ; Wembley Park ; Wembley Wembley Hill or Wembley Stadium   TROLLEYBUS: 662 BUSES: 11 · 18 · 18c · 83; also special service Aldwych to Wembley

Poster for 1937 Cup Final

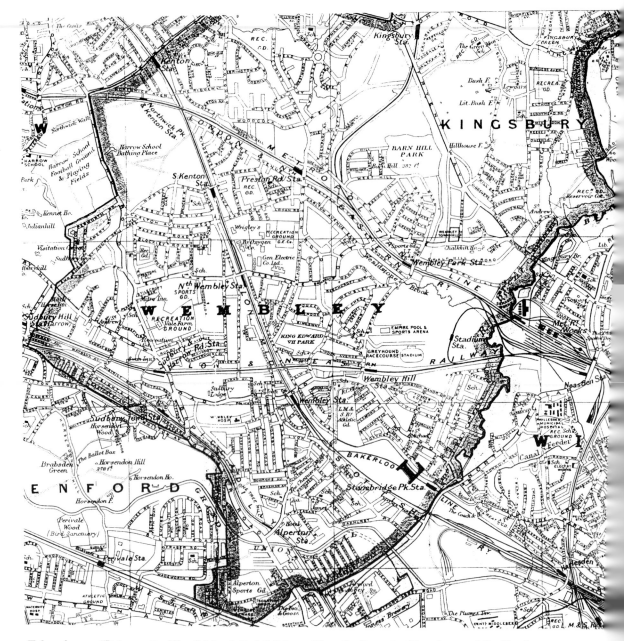

Taken from a "Between the Wars" Municipal Edition of Stanford's map of London and its Environs.

Wembley

All over the world the name 'Wembley' suggests sport, concert or pageant. Although some would like to challenge its pre-eminence, for many, sportsmen in particular, the 'road to Wembley' remains the route to the top, to the ultimate victory. Wembley is an icon to millions who know nothing of the rather indeterminate, very middling, middle place of 'semis', geographically and socially between the warmth and noise of the inner suburbs and the laurels and golf clubs of Northwood and Moor Park. But, by an irony, this scene of the last great exhibition of the British Empire is now home to a kaleidoscope of people who were affected and scattered by the death of imperialism – Pakistanis, Indians, Bangladeshis and Irish to whom the minutiae of Anglican churches and afternoon teas of Betjeman's former Middlesex are of small concern. Nevertheless the morning trains are still loaded with commuters travelling to the traditional business of London as they have since Metroland was in its green infancy.

For the purposes of our text when we refer to Wembley we shall, in general, mean the area of the one-time Borough; in fact, Wembley has had a curiously fluctuating administrative history. At the beginning of the nineteenth century Wembley was a part of the parish of Harrow and its population by 1851 was a mere 203. Under the Local Government Act of 1894 Wembley became an Urban District, with some misgivings on the part of the inhabitants of Kingsbury which in 1897 was a 'separate associated area' and by 1901 was established as a completely independent Urban District. This lasted until 1934 when Kingsbury was incorporated once more into Wembley U.D.C.

By 1937 with a large and increasing population Wembley acquired the status of Municipal Borough, and in 1965 the boroughs of Wembley and Willesden were fused to create the new borough of Brent, which made its headquarters at the former Wembley Town Hall in Forty Lane.

Although Wembley is often spoken of as a suburb development of the twenties and thirties, its component settlements – Alperton, Preston and Sudbury – had Victorian estates at the core of their communities. Unfortunately, over-eager developers destroyed several of the older and more interesting buildings, at a time when there was little statutory protection for or public interest in the heritage of smaller, domestic architecture. After the watershed of 1924/5 change came apace. In 1934 the Wembley Arena opened as a giant swimming pool that could be converted into an ice rink and floored over to accommodate various indoor sports. In the early 1970s the Wembley Conference Centre with a main auditorium seating 2,700 was constructed, providing a new and important focus for traffic and travel in the Borough.

As this book is being published the country is waiting for the Sports Council's final decision as to whether England's new stadium will be at Manchester or on the site of the existing Wembley Stadium which will then be demolished.

LENS OF SUTTON

*'Three views of
Sudbury and Wembley,
now Wembley Central,
c.1907*

LENS OF SUTTON

The LNWR–LMS–Bakerloo

The first railways in Middlesex were not 'short' local lines but main trunk routes, commencing with the London and Birmingham. Looking at the first one-inch Ordnance Survey map with its later railway additions to 1891 the LNWR is shown clearly running through apparently virgin countryside from Willesden to Watford. There is a station at Harrow (some distance to the north of the established community of Harrow-on-the-Hill) but 'Wembley' scarcely exists; the map shows a big expanse for "Wembly Park" with Hill Cottage and Oakington Farm on its boundaries, and away to the west the "Swan" public house towards Sudbury – and little else. The 'Paddington Canal'* meanders away to the south and there are tiny settlements at Preston, Kingsbury and Alperton.

Harrow not only had its station earlier than Sudbury/Wembley but was earlier to receive the advantages and disadvantages of railway development. (Curiously, Harrow School, in the interests of the morals and discipline of its scholars, wished the first station to be at Wembley – i.e. as far away from the school as possible – but did not make its protest until Harrow station, initially titled Harrow Weald station, had, in fact, been erected).

The London and Birmingham combined with the Grand Junction and the Liverpool and Manchester railways on 16th July 1846 to form the LNWR.

In 1858 the LNWR offered a first-class season free for eleven years for commuters from Harrow to London if they were occupiers of new houses with over £50 annual rateable value. A very early casualty is recorded on a tombstone in Harrow churchyard:

"Bright rose the morn and vigorous rose poor Port
Gay on the train he used his wonted sport,
Ere noon arrived his mangled form they bore
With pain distorted and overwhelmed with gore
When evening came to close the fatal day
A mutilated corpse the sufferer lay."

The London and Birmingham had been opened first from Euston to Boxmoor in July 1837. The two track main line was soon congested by ever-increasing traffic, and an up goods line was added in 1858 between Watford and Primrose Hill tunnel. By 1875 the same section had been quadrupled.

Wembley's first station (as opposed to lineside stopping place) opened in 1845 as Sudbury, changed to Sudbury and Wembley on 1st April 1882, altered again on 1st November 1910 to Wembley for Sudbury, reflecting the growing importance of Wembley, and, at last, on 5th July 1948, coinciding with the first post-war Olympics, held at Wembley, the Sudbury part of the title disappears and the station becomes Wembley Central.

Despite the season ticket offer at Harrow, the LNWR did little to stimulate building along its lines for the first half-century of the railway era, for two reasons: they concentrated

*The 'Paddington Canal' now the Paddington Arm of the Grand Union Canal was when it was opened in 1801, one of Wembley's earliest 'modern' transport provisions. The Canal now crosses the North Circular Road at Alperton by an aqueduct built in the 1930s, which burst in 1962 causing serious flooding. The River Brent feeds the Welsh Harp which is an important water supplier for the Canal. The canal feeder wanders southward to the east of the River Brent and the Wembley boundary. Passenger fly-boats provided a service on the Canal in a fashion accurately portrayed in C.S. Forester's "Hornblower and the 'Atropos'".

on the more profitable long distance traffic, and their London terminus was not very conveniently situated for the City or Westminster. In particular, the LNWR was less than enthusiastic about the provision of parliamentary trains for the poorer working classes. An LCC enquiry of 1892 found the response of the LNWR (and the GWR) to the Cheap Trains Act of 1883 had been unsatisfactory, exemplifying the Willesden area for the paucity of provision.

Nevertheless, the original settlement of Wembley lies on the High Road about Wembley Central station; the Metropolitan Railway, as we shall see, did not provide a Wembley Park station until 1894 fourteen years after its line was constructed through the district. Wembley, a hamlet of Harrow parish until 1894, had a population of 10,277 in 1881, 31,217 in 1911 and 124,843 in 1961.

'The Railway Mania' of 1845-6 produced a crop of generally sterile railway proposals for Middlesex. The Buckinghamshire Railway scheme included a southern Aylesbury to Harrow section designed to traverse the Wembley area via the "Black Horse" in Oldfield Lane, alongside Horsenden Lane North, across the northern part of Horsenden Wood in a cutting, and parallel to Harrow Road, crossing over Ealing Road near the library. There was to have been a junction with the LNWR south of what is now Wembley Central station. This part of the Buckinghamshire Railway project was rejected by Parliament in 1846.

In 1864 a survey was undertaken for a London, Harrow & Rickmansworth Railway which would have its southern terminus at a junction with the LNWR at Stonebridge Park, from whence it would have climbed to Alperton, then crossed the Grand Junction Canal in two places, uniting with another branch of the LH & R. Rly which gave access to the GWR near West London Junction. The combined line would have run over Brabsden Green and Oldfield Lane and out to Roxeth, Pinner and Rickmansworth.

The London and Aylesbury Railway, incorporated in 1871 also included a projected southern section from the LNWR at Rickmansworth to a junction close to Ruislip Reservoir, one line running south to the Great Western adjacent to its Uxbridge terminus, the other to Greenford Green south of the "Swan" public house at Sudbury and again to meet the LNWR at the north end of Sudbury station. The L & A Rly collapsed in 1874.

It is interesting that few of these early pipe-dreams mention a place called Wembley; it was merely an eastern portion of Harrow.

The initial train service at Sudbury in 1842* was but two trains in each direction – to Euston at 8.44 am and 9.58 am ; to Aylesbury via Cheddington at 3.20 pm and to Wolverton at 6.20 pm. In 1845 there were only three down and five up local trains each weekday and three each way on Sundays. Only one train a day took third class passengers. In 1879 after the main line was quadrupled, an hourly Euston to Watford basic service was instituted, with substantially increased peak-time provision.

Although, until the 1930s Wembley's post offices were sub-offices of Harrow, Wembley's association with the Royal Mail came early. It is recorded that an allowance of £1 per year for wax and string was paid to the Station Master at "Sudbury" for two years from 1st April 1867. From January 26th, 1875 he was given a more comprehensive allowance of 3/- per week for "the conveyance of bags in connection with the Night Mail to the North". Already, mail to destinations outside London could be bagged and deposited on the London to Birmingham, Holyhead and Chester trains.

---

*It appears that trains may have stopped at Sudbury prior to the erection of a proper station building. It was not until 1st June 1842 that an expenditure of £180 was approved for a station at Harrow Road bridge (i.e. Sudbury). "The intermediate stations (of the London & Birmingham Railway) call for little notice, most of the roadside stations being modest affairs with no platforms, passengers entering or leaving the trains on both sides." W. L. Steel 'History of the LNWR;' 1914.

"Sudbury and Wembley" station had three platforms, with a small booking office perched on the road above (then clear of building for some distance either way) across the southernmost running lines. A covered and glazed walkway crossed the northern two lines, and covered stairs descended to the three platforms, which stretched from the road towards London. Flat-roofed canopies covered about a quarter of the platforms, although the canopy on the southernmost was shorter than the others and a house for the station master adjoined it.

The 1880s saw a proposal for a new Harrow, Ealing and Willesden line which although ultimately aborted, was of particular interest in the context of Wembley's transport history

This owed its origins to Henry Haynes, the Alperton businessman, who in 1885 approached George Leane and William Bell to act as engineer and Parliamentary agent for a railway from Willesden, via Alperton, Perivale and Northolt, to Uxbridge. This soon foundered through lack of support. These two men were again retained in October 1886 for a line from Willesden to South Harrow, with a branch from Alperton to Ealing. The promoters were Arthur Horne, chairman of the company developing the Harrow Mount Estate which was partly built but not flourishing because of its remoteness from a station, Joseph Mitchell of Bolton Hall, Rotherham, and Robert Cooper, another stranger to the district. The original list also included R. G. Regerson, a civil engineer from Carlisle, but his name was deleted in favour of Alexander Carlyon who had recently inherited 180 acres in Wembley and Harrow on the death of his uncle and moved to Alperton Lodge from Cornwall.

The line began at a junction with the LNWR west of Willesden Junction running parallel and to the north of it. There would also have been a connecting spur to the Midland Railway Cricklewood-Acton line near Glynfield House. At the point where the LNWR main line crossed the Brent at Stonebridge Park, the HE & WR. would have passed right through the 61ft span arch, which would have involved widening the bridge or diverting the river. The route then ran south west as far as Alperton from which station it closely followed the present Piccadilly Line route as far as a terminus below the Gasworks at South Harrow. There would have been an intermediate station by the "Rising Sun" in Greenford Road. From Alperton, a branch was to have run to the increasingly residential district of Castlebar Park.

As this time Harrow was an exclusive residential town with a population of 11,000 while Ealing had much better shopping and commercial facilities for its 21,000 inhabitants. The HE & WR planned to build just over 7 miles of double track for £250,000, with capital from the deposit loaned by the Alliance Life Assurance Co. The steam-hauled underground trains of those days were not entirely popular, and the promoters envisaged a "daylight route" to Broad Street, via both Chalk Farm and the North London Railway. The spur to the Midland line gave access to St. Pancras also, with the possibility of reaching Moorgate via the Metropolitan widened lines. The promoters' aspirations even extended to through trains to the London, Chatham and Dover Railway, via Farringdon Street. Standing orders of Parliament for the HE & WR Bill were found and complied with on January 21st 1887 and on February 8th it received its second reading. Also on February 8th, Carlyon chaired a meeting of some fifty local landowners in Harrow Public Hall to gain both financial and moral support. John Baker, the railway's solicitor assured them of a return on their capital in a few years' time, and Leane described the route. The meeting ended by passing unanimously a resolution that the local landowners and residents supported the railway.

The evidence of the witnesses supporting the scheme was heard on March 22nd and 23rd, 1887. No less than three witnesses spoke of goods traffic on the line. Haynes wanted to develop a "great manufacturing district in the north west of London", and already owned about 85 houses and employed over 100 men in Alperton. He sent bricks by canal to places such as Paddington, Camden Town and Lea Bridge and at that time had seven building contracts in central London. Rail connection with his yard would have stimulated trade. Haynes still nursed his Uxbridge proposal, and as a prominent supporter of the HE & WR hoped to extend the Castlebar Park branch to Uxbridge.

Another building contractor, James Kendall of Roxeth, revealed that he had to pay 3/- per cart of building materials delivered from the LNWR station at Harrow and 2/- per cart from the Met. Dewar Watson, of the Sudbury and Harrow Brewery, assured the railway of a traffic of 5-7 tons of coal per week, plus malt supplied from East Dereham in Norfolk. Most of the beer which he produced at Sudbury was for the London market. Other local witnesses were Carlyon himself, Gen. Copland-Crawford of Sudbury Lodge, and John Wooley of Wembley House, with Henry Gibbons of Kent House, representing the Ealing interest.

On March 24th, the House of Commons Select Committee considered the evidence which it had heard. Both the Harrow and the Ealing Local Boards had made objections, though these were of a minor character concerned with roads, footpaths and sewers. A more serious objection came from the LNWR centred upon the planned junction with their main line at Willesden. The Select Committee would not authorise the line with only the circuitous route via Cricklewood and the prospect of further negotiations with the LNWR so the Bill was thrown out.

The LNWR certainly had its critics, both of its business methods and its engineering achievement and one is not entirely reassured by the comment which O. S. Nock quoted with apparent approval:

"North Western porters and guards do their work with military precision, but with a studied nonchalance which is very appropriate to the oldest and most punctual of our railway companies."

The great fabric of sidings and depots developed quickly, although there was little between Wembley and Brent Junction until the 1900s. D. H. F. Meacock writing in "The Railway Magazine" for November 1911 gives a rather breathless account of what had become a powerful dynamo of railway and therefore economic activity (The LNWR was at one time the largest joint-stock corporation in the world).

"On the north side of the river (Brent) over which the Company has, from time to time, had to provide bridges to carry ten lines of rails, are the up reception sidings, which are adjacent to Wembley station. Here 'midst a network of rails with a ceaseless roar of wheels rolling in all directions, one's attention would probably be attracted by a tank shunting engine snorting out in a measured struggle to propel backward a heavy train of 50 or 60 wagons of coal. How slowly it moves! Surely it is capable of better work! But perhaps there is a very good reason for its slow progress. Let us observe what is happening at the other end of the long string of trucks 300 or 400 yards ahead.

Here we find operations of a most interesting nature in progress. A long shunting neck comes into view, and our train is slowly but surely vanishing away into one of the 13 classification roads leading therefrom. On closer inspection, we discover that just before the shunting neck is reached, the rails are suddenly raised on a mound or 'hump' as it is called, and that they dip again as abruptly to the former level.

What is happening is that each wagon or series of wagons for any particular siding (having been previously unhooked from the train by a shunter) increase their speed as soon as the summit of the 'hump' is reached, leaving the train behind, and running on by 'gravity' without any further mechanical aid into the desired classification road."

Watford to Broad Street train of "Oerlikon" stock near South Kenton 1st September, 1954. The Metropolitan line overbridge can be seen in the Background.

4-6-2 46208 "Princess Helena Victoria" on down special passing South Kenton on Easter Monday 19th April 1954.

Top: The modest and retiring booking office at Kenton.

Centre: A 313 emu approaches South Kenton, Summer 1994.

Bottom: Bakerloo train en route for Harrow disappears into the gloom of Wembley Central.

Douglas Stuckey

Douglas Stuckey

By the opening of the 20th century line occupation at peak periods was near to capacity, the long block section of nearly two miles between Wembley Cutting and Harrow No 1 was a local contributory factor. Also competition from trams and the Metropolitan prodded the LNWR into the far-reaching decision in 1906 to build the 'New Line' to Watford.

The section of the New Line from Willesden to Harrow opened on 15th June 1912. New stations were provided at Harlesden, Stonebridge Park, North Wembley, Kenton and Headstone Lane, as well as new platforms at existing stopping places. (South Kenton was not opened until 3rd July 1933).

The stations at Kenton and North Wembley were, as at Wembley, situated usefully beneath roads central to what became busy communities, with booking offices in each case situated on the south side of the bridge at road level and straddling the 'New Lines'. The station structures were efficient enough (they have changed little over the years) and sub-stantially constructed of brick with various offices on both platforms, but of minimum depth no doubt to economise on land purchases. At North Wembley metal supports have been placed at the rear of the up platform presumably to give extra strength to the long slender structure. The stations on this line have a modest reticence to reveal themselves too readily to the intending traveller; one might have anticipated some bolder signposting. Stonebridge Park station has, as we shall see, suffered from more than its fair share of 'slings and arrows' and has been rebuilt more than once, but its position on the North Circular and close to large, long-established housing estates has ensured continuous heavy patronage.

The initial service on the 'New Line' was steam-hauled and North London trains ran on weekdays only, to Harrow from Broad Street; auto-trains of two coach units worked push-and-pull by Webb 2-4-2 radial tanks were introduced between Willesden and Harrow, and there was a fairly sparse irregular service to and from Euston. On the completion of the line through to Watford the time-table changed to a daily service from Euston or Willesden and weekday only peak-period journeys from Broad Street.

When electrification was decided upon it was inevitable that the 630 volt dc system using third and fourth rails would be adopted, as inter-running was envisaged with the Bakerloo, District and Metropolitan lines, all of whom were already using it. The power station erected at Stonebridge Park as part of the electrification programme officially opened on 24th February 1916 prior to the inauguration of the Willesden to Watford electric service by Bakerloo trains on 16th April 1917, supplemented at peak periods by LNWR electric trains from Broad Street. Steam trains to and from Euston continued to run and provided the only Sunday service until 6th July 1919 when Bakerloo trains commenced a seven-day-a-week operation.

Until 14th June 1965 Bakerloo trains continued to run to Watford Junction throughout the day. Then the service was reduced beyond Queens Park to peak hours only, with six trains to and from Watford, and an additional four as far as Harrow only. In October of that year the Watford trains were further cut back to four journeys and in November 1969 the four Harrow trains were eliminated.

The first Bakerloo trains were made up of stock from the Underground lines, including open-ended gated trailers borrowed from the Piccadilly, and were painted in LNWR colours. In 1920-21 new and handsome LNWR/London Electric Company joint stock replaced the borrowed cars. On 7th July 1922 a special inaugural train to celebrate the completion of the 1911 electrification scheme ran from Broad Street to Watford Junction, then to Croxley Shed, returning to Stonebridge Park where after an inspection of the shed and power station the party enjoyed a good lunch before being taken up the line to Euston.

13

On 10th a full daily electric service Euston to Watford Junction commenced, augmented at peak hours by Broad Street commuter workings. Around about 1920, after the construction of an additional two tracks for the New Line from Camden to Queens Park, the LNWR introduced a strange hybrid peak hours only train shuttling between Queens Park and Harrow. The train consisted of two Oerlikon motor coaches with two West Coast Joint Stock Westinghouse-fitted coaches sandwiched between them. Only the leading coach in each direction was 'on power', and the First Class seats were available to allcomers as the train was described as Third Class only.

The opening of the 'New Lines' gave scope for much improved services to the outer commuter areas beyond Watford. A new Watford-Euston non-stop achieved 22 minutes start to stop for the 17½ miles. By 1922, however, only a handful of trains from or to beyond Watford made a stop at Wembley, the rest charging past at up to 75 mph.

Up to the end of the Second World war, apart from a few 'Jinty' 3F 0-6-0Ts and the odd diesel shunter, LNWR engines of the Webb era predominated in local activity. There were 0-6-2T Coal tanks, 18in "Cauliflower" Goods 0-6-0s and the Watford 0-6-2Ts, (which first appeared in 1898 as a development from the "Cauliflowers") the "Coal Tanks" being the most numerous. In the last days of the LMS all the LNWR engines were replaced by Midland railway 2F 0-6-0s but this was a stop-gap measure until construction of small engines recommenced after the War. New Ivatt Class 2 2-6-0s soon arrived, together with both Fowler and Stanier Class 3 2-6-2Ts. All the 2-6-2Ts had gone by 1961, replaced by Class 4 2-6-4Ts which had been cascaded from local passenger work by dieselisation. The Ivatt Class 2s (together with some of the BR standard version) 2-6-4Ts, and the odd 'Jinty' performed this work until the end of steam in September 1965. Diesels used in early days for local work were Class 08 and 11 shunters, Type 1 Class 20s and Type 2 Class 24s. The diesel shunter soon achieved a monopoly of Sudbury sorting sidings.

A familiar sight around Wembley for generations were the old tender engines retained at Watford for departmental use, and given the name-plate "Engineer, Watford". These ranged over the years from a Crewe type 2-2-2 which commenced this duty in 1891 to, in 1936, a 2P class 4-4-0 No 672 which lasted but without the name-plate until 1962.

The first LNWR electric stock for the New Line was four 3-Car sets known as 'Siemens' after the manufacturer of the electrical equipment, not the builder (Metropolitan Carriage and Wagon). Although the Siemens stock used Stonebridge Shed it rarely worked on the Watford route. 75 sets of "Oerlikon" stock were built between 1915 and 1921, named likewise after the manufacturer of the motors and electrical equipment, and again built by MCW, with trailers constructed by the LNWR, was among the most universally popular LMS suburban stock for comfort, space and good riding abilities; albeit that, with two doors on each side, loading and unloading could be tedious (and the fierce electric heaters were a hazard for the bare legs of travelling boys!)

Traffic grew as housing development took place and in 1927 25 additional 3 Car sets were ordered, unlike the original stock they were of conventional compartment design. All Oerlikon stock was withdrawn to 1955-60 and replaced by Class 501 units built at Eastleigh to a design of Southern style. By September 1985 the 501s gave place to Class 313 trains from Eastern Region's Hornsey depot, access being gained to the North London lines by a newly-electrified freight curve at York Road.

Stonebridge Park station was an early casualty being destroyed on 9th January 1917 by fire, remaining closed until 1st August. (It was again a victim of fire damage in September 1945 and was rebuilt in concrete in 1948). On 3rd October 1940 a delayed action bomb caused extensive damage at Stonebridge Park shed; two cars had to be scrapped. Stonebridge Park power station had four Westinghouse turbines coupled to 5,000 kW alternators, giving three phase 25 cycle current at 11,000 volts through BTH switchgear. Two other more powerful sets were added later bringing the total output up to 46,000 kW.

The eastern end of the power station contained the repair shed; in addition to running repairs generally the shed dealt with all repairs to electrical equipment. It was not intended as a a running shed but trains were stabled there during the war years and afterwards in a diminishing way until 1957. During the late thirties a programme for the reconditioning of the power supply had been worked out, and this was carried through under wartime conditions at a reduced rate. Between 1940 and 1946 the power station equipment was modernised and converted to generate at 50 cycles per second with a total rating of 38,000 kilowatts.

In August 1936 the LMS Magazine stated in an article on "The Reconstruction of Wembley Station": "Twenty five years ago Wembley was a comparatively unimportant station on the LNW Railway Company's main line . . .

In order that the LMS services should keep pace with the ever-growing traffic, an extensive scheme of modernisation was embarked upon, and the present LMS station can now be ranked as one of the most attractive of London suburban stations." (In fairness only a prejudiced LMS enthusiast could have entirely endorsed this eulogy).

Situated on the south side of Wembley's main thoroughfare, namely Harrow Road, the station buildings consisted of a footbridge with staircases to each of the four platforms, with a large booking and parcels office at the eastern end, and a smaller booking office at the western end. In addition there was a special roadway from the up slow platform to Harrow Road, this being only used to accommodate cup final crowds, etc. Between the emergency exit and the eastern booking office there was a vacant strip of land. On the north side of Harrow Road there was a brick parapet. In conjunction with the modernisation of the station, the opportunity was taken to develop the frontage and to lease the land for the construction of parades of shops." (Hence the rather obscured appearance of the station entrance).

The bridge was widened by an additional forty feet and the station itself had to be moved back to provide for nine shops on the south side of Harrow Road and the modernisation of the station accommodation. "The magnitude of the work may be judged by the fact that the necessary alterations involved the demolition of about 100 feet of the electric line platforms at the northern end and the lengthening of these platforms by a similar distance at the southern end; the refixing of awnings and the removal to more suitable positions of the stationmaster's office, waiting rooms, porters' rooms etc., to positions farther south; the widening of electric line staircases and the construction of an arcade thirty three wide . . . with a booking office and bookstall . . ."

At the end of 1963 a second major redevelopment took place at Wembley Central. A 2½ acre 'raft' built at road level gave a total 4 acre site for new shops and offices. The raft was a considerable engineering feat requiring over 1,000 piles, each to be sunk to a depth of 60 to 80 feet. The raft had to be completed by June 1964 to avoid interference with nearby electrification for the West Coast scheme. During this operation a temporary station entrance and booking office was provided in Station Grove at the London end of the station with a temporary footbridge to the up platform.

£30,000 was spent on a face-lift in 1983. Through all the changes of name for Wembley's station the signal box just to the south controlling access to the network of sidings retained its name of Sudbury Junction.

The early 1960s saw both the implementation nationally of the sweeping Beeching closures of major branches and alternative routes and, more encouragingly, the promise of the great West Coast and other substantial electrification. Interruptions and alterations to train services through Wembley were frequently necessary during the West Coast work – Birmingham services used Paddington as London terminal, Manchester was reached over Midland metals from St Pancras, and sleeping-car trains (which are greedy of platform occupation) were diverted, two to Kensington Olympia, one to St Pancras and three to Marylebone. Empty stock still had to be worked to and from the normal carriage sidings. Changes to the Watford New Line time-table enabled a quicker turn-round of stock using one Euston platform only, and, at some week-ends, trains were terminated at Primrose Hill. Energising of the overhead wiring from Northampton through to Queen's Park took place on July 19th 1965.

During the commissioning of new signal boxes over the week-end 25th-27th September 1966, 26 main line trains began or ended their journeys at Wembley Central or Marylebone and 14 outer-suburban trains were truncated at Wembley or Primrose Hill.

Early in 1948 the power station was connected to the National Grid and reciprocal arrangements were negotiated with the London Transport power supply system. Special connections to enable mutual support in an emergency were made at West End Lane and Kenton. In 1929 the LMS ordered thirty 40 ton side-discharging coal wagons from the Birmingham Railway Carriage and Wagon Co Ltd, specifically to run between the collieries and Stonebridge Park. There were then severe limitations on handling high-capacity wagons at many collieries but there was a number used by the LMS with screens high enough to accept these new trucks. It was intended that they should run in trains of twelve and that emptying and clearing a train should be completed within 30 minutes. The sloping top and lattice-girder construction of the hopper were designed to give strength without undue weight and, in fact, the tare was a modest 19 tons. Popularly known as the 'tin trucks' they were vacuum brake fitted, were the largest wagons owned by the LMS and made up a very early example of a 'liner' train.

When the idea of a British Empire Exhibition was mooted the Wembley UDC actually opposed the siting of it in the area as it had its own plans for the development of a high-class 'garden suburb'. In the event the Exhibition came, many wealthy owners of large houses left the district and there was a great impetus for industrial as well as housing expansion.

The LMS contribution to transport for the British Empire Exhibition included an all-day Broad Street to Watford service on weekdays. In the summer of of 1925 about half of these trains were diverted to terminate at Croxley Green. Long after the end of the Exhibition this latter service continued to operate, albeit at varying intervals until finally reverting to a peak hours only provision in September 1929.

In 1944 new six-car trains of stock appeared on Bakerloo-Watford services with the curious legend on the sole-bars – 'Property of the LNER'. This stock had been ordered in 1938 in connection with the intended electrification of the LNER suburban lines, and had been released from storage to meet heavy wartime demands.

After the Hitler War the London Plan Working Party, which reported in 1949, suggested that the New Line should be terminated at Harrow, and that Marylebone should be the London terminal for a new outer suburban service which would run down the Great Central as far as Kenton where it would reach the LMS by a new spur and continue out as far as Tring.

It would have been a miracle if over a century and a half of operation of one of the world's busiest stretches of railway there had been neither accident nor misfortune. One

Top: Class 90 No 90006 arrives at Wembley Inter-City Depot on the evening of 8th November, 1988, having completed a successful evaluation test run to Glasgow with the first driving Van Trailer attached to the other end of the train.

Bottom: Class 85 No 85030 prepares to leave Euston with empty coaching stock on 10th November, 1988.

very early memorable incident concerned Herbert Spencer, well known later as a 19th century philosopher – his theories of evolution were published four years ahead of Darwin – but then in August 1838 working as an engineer for the London and Birmingham Railway. Following an assignment surveying Wolverton station he was anxious to return to his home at Wembley. The last train which Spencer could catch was the eight-o-clock London departure scheduled to run non-stop Watford to Euston. Spencer arranged to have a 'slip coach' (a truck without brakes!) to be attached, and released about one and a half miles before Harrow station. The slip took place, but, unfortunately, not sufficient consideration had been given to the gradient and Spencer found himself rumbling forward for a further few miles beyond his Harrow destination, finally coming to a halt on a level just before a siding and the viaduct over the River Brent. After some hurried words of explanation Spencer recruited a dumb-founded crossing-keeper who helped him to push the runaway truck off the main line into safety.

On July 9th 1909 a young athlete, Carl Veigal, was killed when a signalman prematurely switched points under a local train, and a year later a coal merchant, John Pratt, was crushed to death between trucks during a shunting operation.

Two accidents occured during the Hitler War, in 1940 and 1944. The first happened at 7.10 pm on 12th October when the late-running 11.50 am Lime Street to Euston express consisting of 11 bogie coaches and two four wheeled vans drawn by Baby Scot 5529 hit a barrow being manhandled to the down island platform. The barrow carrried about half a ton of bleach ointment destined for the also tardy 6.46 pm parcels train on the down slow. Three (apparently lightly-built) men had almost successfully accomplished the task and were near the top of the 1 in 8 ramp when one of the men slipped and the barrow careered backward stopping with its corner fouling the up line. A porter signalman seeing the express a mere few hundred yards away rushed to telephone the Sudbury Junction signalman in a vain attempt to avert disaster; the driver travelling through the dusk at 55 mph could not have seen the obstruction. Tragically, the first coach not only derailed but fell broadside across the track, rendering a bad accident worse as the rest of the train piled up behind it. The engine and tender ended on their right sides with a rail penetrating the boiler from end-to-end; both enginemen and nine passengers were killed and there were four other serious injuries. By painful irony the engine had struck an object only $1\frac{1}{4}$" in diameter – the rear axle of the barrow. The resulting problems of the accident were accentuated by a subsequent air attack on Queen's Park on 15th/16th October.

A collision took place at North Wembley in 1944 when an electric train of LMS compartment stock which had been tripped and stopped, was restarted after the trip arm had been raised, and collided with the Bakerloo train ahead, damaging motor-coach No 3345.

A worrying and much-discussed accident occured just to the south of Wembley Central station on 11th October, 1984 when the 5.54 pm Euston-Bletchley passenger train ran into a Willesden-Holyhead freightliner carrying a mixed load of chemicals, tar and asphalt. Three people were killed and about sixty injured and, although there was a spate of argument and correspondence as to the cause of the collision, and the passenger train driver seemed ready to accept some responsibility, the investigating officer at a subsequent enquiry pronounced that there was "no clear conclusion" which could explain the lethal incident. The crucial question – was the passenger train's signal ahead at red or green could not be answered with confidence.

In April 1986 a middle aged man and woman were killed when their Cortina car ran out of control in Llanover Road at 8.30 in the evening, plunged on to the rails near North Wembley station and was hit by an eleven coach empty stock train travelling from Watford to Willesden sidings.

Stonebridge Park power station ceased to supply the dc lines from 30th July 1967. Demolition of the power station took place at the end of 1972 and plans were laid for a new depot for the Bakerloo line, needed when the new Fleet/Jubilee line opened and took over the Bakerloo stabling area at Neasden. There were strong protests from the residents of Tokyngton Avenue who envisaged heavy noise and dirt pollution; LT offered to buy thirty properties most at risk, at advantageous prices.

The opening of the new depot coincided with the restoration of Bakerloo passenger services to Stonebridge Park from 1st May 1979 and from 4th June 1984 18 journeys were extended to Harrow.

The formal opening of the new Bakerloo depot (built on former British Railways land) took place on April 9th 1979 when Horace Cutler, Leader of the then GLC unveiled a commemorative plaque. The depot was provided with a main shed and covered sidings each containing six tracks There was a two-track lifting shop and all train movements as well as the washing machine were electronically controlled. Universal radio rather than loudspeaker communication, and the planting of a belt of trees and shrubs were designed to protect the amenities of the local population.

Stonebridge Park has suffered more than its fair share of misfortune. In June 1975 there was another fire at the station destroying wooden waiting rooms which had not been replaced when in 1948 most of the station had been rebuilt in concrete. In the 1980s a railwaywoman was robbed at gunpoint and a railwayman was kidnapped by four youths who wished to rob his home. And at this general period there was much criticism of what the press inevitably dubbed "The Misery Line" (until they used the same soubriquet for the MET when it was under fire!) Confirmed political opponents such as Hugh Dykes MP and Paul Boateng MP found common cause in harrying BR and LT. In 1988 Stonebridge Park was one station nominated by BR for a "face lift". It would be interesting to know how many lines have been christened 'misery lines', their christening to be followed shortly by confirmation of an impending 'face lift' Perhaps a little unexpectedly Stonebridge Park station has been advanced as a modern building whose architecture merits preservation.

At the time of writing there is a weekday 20 minute interval service Euston-Watford supplemented by a 20 minute Bakerloo service as far out as Harrow & Wealdstone – so Wembley which is on the busiest section of the Watford line has a 10 minute interval provision to and from London. Main line trains are frequently stopped additionally at Wembley Central in connection with major sporting and other events; the only regular use of the main line platforms at Wembley is late night and very early morning when a service of Northampton trains is scheduled to call at Harrow as well as Wembley. What had been styled Network South East-North London Lines has with the onset of privatisation been changed to North London Railways operating on former LMR lines as far north as Birmingham. A complex programme of modernisation and alterations is in progress on other parts of this system, to accommodate new routes from the Channel Tunnel to allow for the extension of the Jubilee Line and to provide new and refurbished stations. The Wembley lines are controlled from the Wembley Suburban Signalling Centre and the 313 emus are manned from Watford and St Pancras as well as Wembley depots. Although the name Harlequin line, which had been adopted for promotional purposes, was dropped fairly quickly a logo of coloured diamond shapes remains.

The arrival of privatisation and the opening of the Channel Tunnel spurred vast changes generally, and in the Wembley area in particular. What had been known as the Sudbury sorting sidings just north of Stonebridge Park were transformed into the commodious European Freight Operating Centre, occupying 16 kilometres of track alongside the

RAILFREIGHT DISTRIBUTION

Top: Trains assembling shortly after opening.

Bottom: A general view of the Depot taken at the time of opening with Wembley Central straddling the tracks in the distance.

RAILFREIGHT DISTRIBUTION

West Coast main line with full-length and departure sidings, 5 shorter reception sidings, 6 sorting sidings, 5 holding sidings, 5 locomotive sidings and 1 customs reception siding. The complex is designed to handle up to 70 international timetabled trains daily to and from France, Germany, Italy and Spain, trains with a maximum length of approximately half a mile. Typical best transit times are intended to be of the order of 13 hours to Paris, 30 to Milan and 27 to Perpignan.

Between the European freight depot and Stonebridge Park Underground depot, on the up side of the West Coast main line is situated Wembley Inter-City depot, now operated by Inter-City West Coast under their Fleet Engineer (London) who is responsible for train drivers as well as mechanical engineering. Wembley handles about 300+ passenger coaches and parcels vehicles units for the WCML.

Wembley Inter-City is physically divided by the Euston-Watford dc electric lines. On one side is the heavy repair facility and on the other the maintenance depot. The Heavy Repair depot is the oldest structure, being built in 1915 by First World War prisoners-of-war. As stated earlier, this is the former dc stock maintenance depot and in the Second World War received a coat of camouflage paint, traces of which have resisted the ravages of time. The servicing and cleaning shed was built in 1953 with a two-road maintenance shed following in 1985. BR were proud of their new installation which had been planned by the LMS in 1936 but whose construction had been delayed by the War (when its site had formed an additional temporary goods yard). Cleaning was on an assembly line basis with stock being moved by 'mules', no engine being attached. The latest addition to the Depot was the expensive (£500,000) wheel lathe. It has been found expedient to operate stock on a fixed formation basis and although more difficult to achieve, efforts are made to keep locomotives in the same set formations. Wembley undertakes 'A' examinations but for extensive inspections they have to be sent to Willesden depot. The Wembley work-force numbers about 260 but many of them are doomed to redundancy when Inter-City carries out its threatened closure of the Wembley depot. Work now undertaken there is to be transferred mainly to Polmadie, Glasgow, and the Wembley site will be retained for limited stabling facilities only.

Although railway lines occupied a vast part of the area of Wembley there were few private sidings. One industrial complex partly rail-served lay just to the north of North Wembley station, on the east side of the main line. Here were Wrigley's (chewing gum) British Oxygen Industrial Gases (now reduced to a cylinder exchange depot) and an important clutch of GEC establishments. Of these Osram (lamps) was the biggest, and when rail traffic to that factory ceased in 1969 their 0-4-0 Fowler locomotive "Osram", built as long ago as 1933, was acquired for preservation by two members of the Buckinghamshire Railway Centre at Quainton Road. Osram, originally located at Hammersmith, was half-owned by the German DGA, and GEC purchased the German half from the Trustee of Enemy Property after the First World War. The Osram factory was built in the 1920's in conjunction with the famous Hirst Research establishment, which has now moved to Borehamwood. Osram, itself, now forms part of Siemens Lighting, but the whole East Lane site remains GEC property. The stump of the industrial sidings is still connected to the main line.

Writing in "A Confidential History of the Research Laboratories" in 1945 Doctor C. C. Paterson recollected: "I wonder how many remember the walk or should I say adventure in getting from North Wembley station to the laboratories. The station in those days was only a 'halt' and East Lane was a country lane, muddy and narrow, with a narrow bridge over the railway. Houses had not then been built opposite to us so that from the field on which they now stand we had an uninterrupted view of the facade of the Laboratories". British Oxygen, whose factory lay alongside the main line manufactured potentially hazardous gases such as hydrogen and a close liaison was maintained with the local fire services as a necessary precaution.

Signalling on the 'New Line' was initially manual with signal boxes often forming part of the station structures. It soon proved impossible to cope with increasing traffic and, in 1932, the LMS decided to instal automatic colour-light 'searchlight' signals, and the change-over was completed by February 1933. "Searchlight" is the term for a signal which has a single lamp and lens; the operation of a sliding spectacle plate with appropriate coloured glasses between the lamp and the lens determines which aspect is displayed.

An unusual feature of 'New Line' signalling was an automatic 'calling-on' facility allowing trains to proceed past a stop signal at danger after an interval of 70-80 seconds; if the overlap track circuit was clear the trip arm dropped and the red marker changed to a miniature yellow light.

A similar function applied to repeater signals. Alert vigilance was essential as, in the case of prolonged signal failure or line obstruction, several trains could find themselves buffer to buffer in the same section. This system lasted over fifty years but by the 1980s it was obsolete and troublesome, and a brand new set of signals was put in place. Train services were suspended over the week-end 10/11th December 1988 to allow the switching out and replacement of the old system.

After West Coast electrification in the 1960s it was necessary to instal electronic circuits to counter interference between the 630 volt DC fourth rail electric lines and the new 25kv 50 cycle AC main line system. From July 1964 a new box at Watford Junction controlled the 28 route miles between North Wembley and Cheddington, replacing 14 mechanical signal boxes. A new Willesden box for the section North Wembley to South Hampstead came into operation from July 11th 1965.

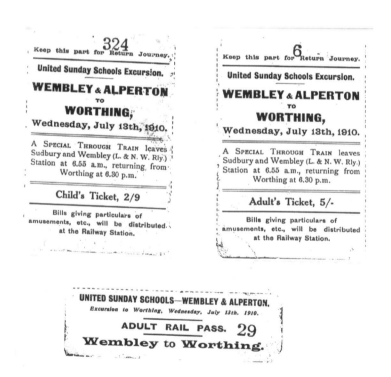

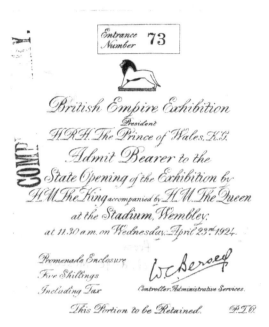

The Stadium Terrace

Replica of GWR "North Star" photographed 26th September, 1925.

LNWR 2-2-2 "Columbine" No. 49 – Built in 1845 for the Grand Junction Railway, as rebuilt with cab and Webb chimney. Now at National Railway Museum, York.

"Flying Scotsman" arriving at the Exhibition with three cars of the Never-Stop Railway passing in the background.

Southern Railway N Class 2-6-0 A 866 in the Palace of Engineering.

H. C. CASSERLEY

The LMS 4-6-0 5845 was built by Beardmore's in 1924 and was named " Prince of Wales" temporarily when exhibited. This view was taken later at Crewe.

W. POTTER

A general view with Royal National Lifeboat Institution Pavilion in the left background with the Stadium behind it.

The Commonwealth of Australia Pavilion built in the rather heavily authoritarian style typical of many Exhibition buildings.

The Metropolitan Railway

The Metropolitan Railway's activities at Wembley Park make an interesting story, with many developments, from Sir Edward Watkin's abortive attempt to imitate the Eiffel Tower in the 1890s through to the opening of the Stanmore branch some forty years later.

The original Metropolitan Railway linking the Great Western Railway at Paddington with the City was opened in 1863. A branch line was opened from Baker Street to Swiss Cottage in 1868 and this formed the beginning of its "Extension Line" into the open fields of Middlesex, ultimately reaching Verney Junction in far-off Buckinghamshire. The section through Wembley was opened from Willesden Green to Harrow-on-the-Hill on August 2nd, 1880 with just one intermediate station at Kingsbury Neasden (the present Neasden). Preston Road was opened as a halt on May 21st, 1908 and was rebuilt into a station which came into use on November 22nd 1931; Northwick Park had no station until June 28th, 1923.

Sir Edward, Chairman of the Metropolitan from 1872 to 1894, paid a visit to Paris and was very impressed with the Eiffel Tower, whose receipts during 1889, its first year, were said to have repaid more than two thirds of its initial cost. He and some of his Metropolitan Railway associates decided that London needed a similar edifice, so on August 14th 1889 the Tower Company was formed, with Sir Edward as Chairman and an authorised capital of £200,000, increased in July 1890 to £300,000, with borrowing powers not to exceed £150,000. A competition was held to find the best design for the Tower and 68 entries were received, the first prize being won by Stewart, McLaren & Dunn. A site had now to be chosen, and many were suggested, including one almost opposite Kings Cross station, and a site near Ladywell station on the South Eastern Railway.

Wembley Park was eventually chosen, however. This was hardly surprising, as the Park, which extended over part of Wembley Hill and as far as the River Brent towards Neasden, had been purchased by the Metropolitan Railway in 1889. It was considered that, situated here, wonderful views of London could be had from the Tower, and that the Park would also become a popular pleasure resort. The Tower Company appointed Sir Benjamin Baker as Engineer in November 1890; Sir Henry Oakley and Charles Scotter, General Managers of the Great Northern and the London & South Western Railways respectively, were asked to stand for election as directors, but both refused.

The contract for the Tower foundations went to J.T. Firbank, of Railway Approach, London Bridge, the contractor who had built the extension of the Metropolitan Railway from Rickmansworth to Chesham, opened on July 8th 1889, and who became a director of the Tower Company on July 1st 1890. The construction of the Tower itself was entrusted to Heenan & Froude of Manchester. A separate firm, the International Tower Construction Co. Ltd., was formed on August 13th 1891 to deal with the erection of the Tower; this was renamed the Metropolitan Tower Construction Co. Ltd. two months later. 124 acres of land at Wembley Park were leased to the Construction Co. for 999 years from December 25th 1891 for £2,000 per annum, and work began on building the Tower, which was to be 1,150 ft high (taller than its rival in Paris!), and would have three platforms, with restaurants, theatres, dancing rooms, Turkish baths and rooms for exhibiting "all kinds of scientific and amusing novelties".

In the meantime, the Metropolitan had signed a contract with Firbank for a station to serve Wembley Park. A siding for receiving construction materials was brought into use in July 1890; during excavations for the station the fossilised remains of a hippopotamus were discovered. The new station had two platforms to the west of the present Bridge Road, with the booking office on the road bridge. It was inspected by Major-General C.S. Hutchinson for the Board of Trade on October 3rd 1893; he stated that in connection with the Wembley Tower then in course of construction, large additions to its facilities were contemplated. There does not appear to have been any ceremonial opening, but the station was used for football matches on October 14th and 21st 1893, the ground in the Park having been leased to the Westminster Football Club.

The Metropolitan evidently expected good public support for the amenities at Wembley Park, and at the end of 1893 the enlarging of the station, forecast by Major-General Hutchinson, was put in hand. This involved widening the up platform to form an island also serving down local trains, laying in new up and down local tracks, a new up local platform, carriage sidings, an engine siding and a new 70-lever signal box at the London end of the station. Goods sidings were also provided, and another siding led into the Park to convey materials for building the Tower. Major-General Hutchinson inspected these additional works on May 8th 1894. Besides making several stipulations regarding signalling, he also required that part of the curve on the up local line be check-railed. He also ruled that shelter should be provided on the new up local platform, within three months. Subject to this and to the signalling alterations being completed in a fortnight, he recommended the opening of the station, which took place, on weekdays only, on May 12th 1894, which was the date of the experimental opening of the Wembley Park grounds to the public. The time limit for the erection of the shelter on the up local platform was subsequently extended to six months. The cost of the roof over Platforms 1 and 2 at Wembley Park was estimated at £2,600, with a further £300 for a waiting room and roof for Platform 3.

In order to accommodate the Great Central's London Extension from Harrow-on-the-Hill, the Metropolitan built two additional tracks, opened in 1898, to Canfield Place, near Finchley Road, for the sole use of the Great Central, the latter building its own tracks to its new terminus at Marylebone. The two additional Metropolitan lines were laid on the down side of the existing tracks; the layout of Wembley Park station was not affected, but the new lines separated the Met. goods yard from its main line, so it was part of the agreement that the Metropolitan should build a connection which crossed the new tracks and connected with its goods yard and with the siding into the Wembley Tower grounds. This siding was removed in 1909, but the connection to the Metropolitan goods yard was retained, though at that time the yard was little used, and its retention was one of the conditions of the Metropolitan & Great Central Joint Committee, formed in 1906.

Freight traffic at Wembley Park gradually expanded, from 2,166 tons in 1914 to 16,026 in the first ten months of 1923, which needed doubling of the yard's capacity by the addition of two more roads, completed early in 1924. Livestock traffic could be handled there.

In the meantime, several steps were taken by the Tower Company with.a view to making Wembley Park an attractive pleasure ground. It was laid out with cricket and football grounds, a running track, a lake with boating house and artificial waterfall, fountains pavilions, tea pagodas and bandstands. Trotting meetings were held from 1899 to 1906, and a cycle track was also constructed. The Tower itself was completed as far as the first platform, 200 ft. up, but after this things hung fire, as the Tower Construction Co. had only been able to raise £27,000 in capital, though the Metropolitan had subscribed a further £60,000. The completed stage of the Tower was opened to the public in May 1896, but

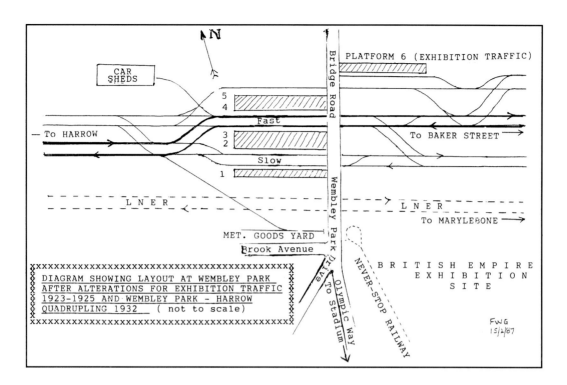

DIAGRAM SHOWING LAYOUT AT WEMBLEY PARK
AFTER ALTERATIONS FOR EXHIBITION TRAFFIC
1923-1925 AND WEMBLEY PARK - HARROW
QUADRUPLING 1932   (not to scale)

N

CAR SHEDS

5
4

Fast

To HARROW

3
2

Slow

1

PLATFORM 6 (EXHIBITION TRAFFIC)

To BAKER STREET

L N E R

L N E R
To MARYLEBONE

MET. GOODS YARD

Brook Avenue

Bridge Road

Wembley Park Drive

Olympic Way To Stadium

NEVER-STOP RAILWAY

B R I T I S H   E M P I R E
E X H I B I T I O N
S I T E

FWG
15/2/87

So far and no further – the Watkin Tower prior to 1907.

during the year, although 104,000 people visited the Park, only 18,500 of them thought it worth while to pay to take the lifts up to the finished platform.

Still further additions to the Park's amenities failed to lure large numbers of Londoners through its turnstiles; 12,000 fewer people came in 1900 than had done in the previous year. In 1906 it was decided to change the title of the Tower Company to the Wembley Park Estate Co., in view of the intention to develop the Park as a housing estate. More cricket and football grounds were added in 1907, together with tennis courts, but when a variety hall which had been opened was seriously damaged by fire in 1911 it was not thought worthwhile to restore it. This hall had been used as one of the earliest British film studios. In 1910 Robert H. Selbie, the Secretary of the Estate Co. and later General Manager of the Metropolitan Railway, reported a deficit of £1,311 (weekly receipts in 1907 and 1908 had varied between £14-16-3d (£14.81) and 9d.(4p)!). He said the Park was too far from London to attract a large number of people as a pleasure resort, and the buildings and fences were in a very bad state of repair, little having been spent on them for several years.

Another reason for the poor support for the Park may have been the existence of a rival, not very far away, in the shape of the Pleasure Gardens at the Welsh Harp Inn, which adjoined the Brent Reservoir at Hendon. These gardens were laid out in the 1860s, and so well established by the time the amenities at Wembley Park were opened; they included a racecourse, boating and fishing on the reservoir, and skating on the latter when it froze over during the severe winters of the last quarter of the 19th Century. The Midland Railway opened a station at Welsh Harp, about 300 yards from the Inn, on the Edgware Road, and on Easter Monday 1881 trains brought about 5,500 people to the Harp. Later that year there were ascents by the Balloon Society of Great Britain. Many music hall artists used to perform at the Inn.

The construction of the Wembley Tower above the 200ft level was never resumed, and at an Extraordinary General Meeting in 1897 the Tower Construction Company decided to go into voluntary liquidation; its assets, such as they were, were transferred to the parent Tower Company. In August 1906 a contract was signed with Heenan & Froude, who had built the completed part of the Tower, to demolish it, and this was completed the following year, Heenan & Froude paying £1,200 for the scrap value of the steelwork. So solidly built was the structure that it had to be removed with explosives – an ignominious end to Watkin's dream of a rival for the Eiffel Tower.

The siding into the Tower grounds was used in 1899 for electrification trials, using a four-rail d.c. system under the supervision of Thomas Parker, an electrical consultant and contractor. Current for this was generated by Met "A" Class 4-4-0 tank No.1, which had been laid aside two years earlier after an accident. This was mounted on blocks, and two coaches similar to "Bogie" steam stock were built at Neasden for use in the experiment, which lasted about a year. The dismantled parts of the Tower were moved out over the siding in 1907, and the siding itself was removed two years later; the two Metropolitan Peckett saddle-tank engines were probably used in these operations.,

There had been several interesting proposals for railways to serve the Park, the most remarkable of which was from the Lartigue Railway Co. to build a monorail system similar to the Listowel & Ballybunion Railway in Ireland, but worked by electric traction; in the same year, 1893, a switchback railway was suggested, and two years earlier Kerr Stuart & Co. had put forward a plan for a 2 ft gauge line. Nothing came of any of these projects however; the switchback was rejected on the grounds that it would spoil the amenities of the Park. There was some sporadic housing development in the grounds, but this was very slow, and by the end of 1915 only 125 houses had been put up.

The British Empire Exhibition

A new lease of life opened up for Wembley Park in 1922, however, when the bulk of the estate, 126 acres, was sold to the British Empire Exhibition authorities. An exposition of this type was first mooted as an Imperial Industries Exhibition in 1902 and the scheme was revived in 1913, but the Great War intervened before anything positive could result. However, on June 13th 1920 the British Empire Exhibition Incorporated was formed (later renamed The British Empire Exhibition (1924) Inc.) An Act of Parliament authorised the Government to contribute up to £100,000 to the Guarantee Fund against any loss sustained by the Exhibition.

The Exhibition was to be held from April to October 1924; the Prince of Wales was President of the General Committee, and David Lloyd George (the Premier), Stanley Baldwin and Admiral Jellicoe were members of the Executive Council. King George V was Patron. Its objects were (1) to boost production of commodities, timber, fruit, grain etc., and especially fisheries; (2) to make the peoples of the Empire better known to each other; (3) to show what was being done to conquer disease and unhealthy conditions – housing and sanitation would be given special prominence; (4) to enable established industries to show what they had to offer and new industries to attract attention by proving what they could do. Provision would be made for "the representation of the Indian Empire and the Overseas Dominions, and their pavilions". A major feature would be the National Sports Ground, which would accommodate upwards of 125,000 spectators, with seats for 30,000. This would possess "some striking architectural features reminiscent in some degree of Greek and Roman stadia" (these quotes are from the official handbook, issued about 1921). The scheme was officially launched at a meeting at the Mansion House on June 7th 1920; the British Empire Exhibition (1924) Inc. had offices at 16 Hobart Place, London, S.W.1.

In a memo to the Metropolitan board on July 27th 1922 Selbie, the Met. General Manager, recommended that Wembley Park station should be enlarged to cater for extra traffic engendered by the forthcoming Exhibition. He suggested (1) The construction of an independent Exhibition platform, 420 ft long, to the east of the existing platforms, with separate booking offices and entrance from the road bridge (2) Lengthening of the existing platforms westwards to 400 ft, and widening of the staircases leading down to them, and (3) The rebuilding of the existing booking offices. The board authorised these new works, and the tender of £14,334 from the Unit Construction Co. Ltd., of 168 Regent Street, London, W.1, was accepted, the work to be completed within 15 weeks from December 11th 1922, so that the new facilities would be ready for the 1923 F.A. Cup Final, which was to be played at the new stadium on April 28th. Further alterations to the station, including provision of some shops in the new station building, were authorised later, at an estimated cost of £2,500; this work went to the same contractors. The Westinghouse Brake & Saxby Signal Company's tender for the provision of automatic signalling was accepted.

Colonel Pringle of the Ministry of Transport inspected the new station on February 16th 1923; two new booking offices had been built on the level of the road bridge over the railway, one serving the original platforms, and the other for the new Exhibition platform. The works had been completed on time, but overtime and weekend working had increased the contract price to £16,600.

The new station, designed by C.W. Clark, the Metropolitan's architect, is a single-storey building in a quite attractive domestic style, with brick and stucco elevation. At each end and at the centre of the road frontage is a wide entrance. surmounted by a canopy with a hipped, tiled roof; thus ample access was presumably provided to cater for crowds visiting the Empire Exhibition. An emblem reading ""M.R. 1923" is displayed on the station frontage. When the station was rebuilt in 1948 for the Olympic Games the exterior of the street level buildings was largely unaltered; but the interior was rebuilt in the 1980s and the booking office resited.

In a public statement in April 1924 Lord Aberconway, the Metropolitan Chairman, said that the company had spent over £50,000 on improving and enlarging the station "so that we may say that everything possible has been done to attract the Wembley traffic to the Metropolitan Railway. We can bring people right into the Exhibition grounds within about 11 minutes. Our arrangements with regard to the Football Cup Tie last April (1923) were tested, and although there was a great deal of complaint about the organisation of the Stadium, our traffic was carried in a way that was quite admirable . . . Mr Holt and our traffic officers, whose arrangements on that occasion deserve the highest praise, tell me that they can cope with all the the traffic which we expect to get from the Exhibition and from the Cup Tie. From the new platforms and booking hall there is a covered way direct into the Exhibition grounds. The Exhibition authorities are constructing what is known as a "never-stop" railway round the Exhibition grounds; that will be connected with the booking hall of our station and will be a valuable feeder to our line".

About 2,000 men were employed by Sir Robert McAlpine & Co. in building the Stadium, a reinforced concrete structure, and this was finished in time for the F.A. Cup Final, already mentioned, between Bolton Wanderers and West Ham, to be played there on April 28th 1923. Something went wrong with the admission arrangements, and a crowd estimated at 200,000 was either admitted or forced their way into the Stadium. Some of these invaded the pitch, and the game had to be held up until a single mounted policeman on a white horse gently shepherded them back onto the terraces or to the exits. Many thousands of spectators failed to gain admittance to the stadium and decided to return home. The Metropolitan had made special arrangements to cope with the heavy traffic of the Cup Final and the Exhibition, including improved signalling between Baker Street and Wembley Park. It was estimated that on Cup Final day the Met. carried 68,000 down and 84,000 up passengers. Reporting to the Board, Selbie, the Metropolitan general manager, said that the new arrangements at Wembley Park, though severely tested, had proved satisfactory, though he recommended that two extra lay-by sidings should be provided, and track alterations to allow trains arriving at Platform 3 to depart from that platform without the necessity of shunting. The Board approved these new works.

The Metropolitan, always good at publicity, decided to have a stand of their own at the Exhibition. Frank Pick, of the Underground Group, suggested that the Met. and the other Underground railways should have a joint stand, but this was politely declined by Selbie, as the Met. had already gone some way with plans for their own stand. This would be in the Transport Section, and 1,200 ft. of space had been reserved. Metropolitan exhibits would include a new First Class electric saloon driving trailer, a model railway (later deleted as being too costly), a colour light, point motor and other signalling items, and model houses showing the activities of Metropolitan Railway Country Estates Ltd., a subsidiary dedicated to promoting housing development on land adjoining Met. stations. The driving trailer, which was not shown as being First Class while at the Exhibition, was built by the Metropolitan Carriage & Wagon Co., and was similar to the stock introduced in 1921 for the Circle Line. The Metropolitan agreed to purchase it at the close of the Exhibition at its cost price of £3,900, the manufacturers promising to pay part of the cost of its space in the Transport Pavilion if they were allowed to publicise, on its stand, the fact that they had built the vehicle. This trailer, which later became London Transport No.6557, afterwards ran on the East London Line, marshalled between two experimental motor cars built in 1925 (L.T. Nos. 2598 and 2599). It survived until 1950.

When the Exhibition reopened in April 1925, electric locomotive No.15 joined the other Metropolitan exhibits, with the panelling removed from one side to show the electrical equipment; it was specially painted, with the trucks and suspension finished in white.

Other locomotives shown at the Exhibition included GWR 4-6-0 No.4073 "Caerphilly Castle", LNER 4-6-2 No.4472 "Flying Scotsman" (it was the juxtaposition of these two engines which seems to have sparked off the Great Western – LNER locomotive exchanges of 1925), Stockton & Darlington Railway 0-4-0 "Locomotion", LMS 4-6-0 No.5845, (temporarily named "Prince of Wales" and specially built for the Exhibition by William Beardmore & Co. with outside Walschaerts valve gear). LMS Horwich-built 4-6-4 tank No.11114, LNWR 2-2-2 "Columbine" of 1845, Furness Railway "Old Coppernob" 0-4-0 No.3, Southern Railway Maunsell "N" Class 2-6-0 No. A866, the Reid-McLeod turbine locomotive, built by the North British Locomotive Co., a three-cylinder oil-burning locomotive for the Buenos Aires Great Southern Railway by Armstrong Whitworth & Co., and a Metropolitan-Vickers electric locomotive built for the Union of South Africa Railways. When the Exhibition re-opened in 1925 the GWR replaced "Caerphilly Castle" with No.4079 "Pendennis Castle".

There were also several railway exhibits in the Indian Pavilion, including models of locomotives and rolling stock from eleven different companies. On one side of the Canadian Pavilion the Canadian National Railways were represented, and the Canadian Pacific system on the other. In 1927, when the Metropolitan electric locomotives received names, No.15 was dubbed "Wembley 1924", with the nameplates surmounted by a replica of the Wembley lion.

Some interesting locomotives were loaned to Neasden LNER engine shed for use in moving exhibits in and out of the Exhibition site. These included two ex-Great Eastern 0-4-0 steam tram engines from Wisbech, Nos. 0125 and 0129, which were at Neasden from December 1924 to May 1925; Staveley shed lent ex-GCR "J62" Class 0-6-0T No.885 from November 1924 to August 1925, and for the final site clearance after the close of the 1925 season ex-NER "Y7" 0-4-0T No.8089 was borrowed from Tyne Dock.

The first sod of the Empire Exhibition was turned by the Duke of York in January 1922. In March of that year a special train, consisting of five "Dreadnought" coaches hauled by an electric locomotive, was worked from Baker Street to Wembley Park and back for the benefit of people who wished to see a mammoth excavator at work in the Exhibition grounds. The Exhibition was opened by King George V and Queen Mary on April 23rd 1924; in terms of visitors it was a great success, and over seventeen million people passed through its turnstiles in 1924. The exhibits on the 216-acre site were many and varied, from recreations of African villages and a replica of the Taj Mahal, to a scale model of a West Indian waterfall. There were vast Palaces of Engineering and of Industry. One of the most popular sections was the amusement park, where America introduced the first dodgem cars and a roller coaster. The Exhibition closed on November 1st 1924, but reopened in April 1925, when among the exhibits was Henry Ford's assembly line for mass producing cars.

Perhaps because the novelty was rather wearing off, the Exhibition was less successful in 1925 than in the previous year, total attendance falling to nearly ten million, a decrease of 44%. The Metropolitan's share of this traffic showed, in financial terms, a reduction of 57%; this was greater than the decrease in attendance because from June 22nd 1925 the Met. had reduced the return fare from Baker Street from 1/3d (6p) to 1/- (5p). However, the whole operation had been a great success for the Metropolitan; in 1924 11,500,000 passengers used Wembley Park station, with 650 trains daily between Baker Street and Wembley Park, the fastest of these doing the journey in ten minutes. In all, 107,250 trains

Wembley Park.

A beautiful RESIDENTIAL ESTATE is rapidly developing in this picturesque and healthy locality which is served by an unrivalled train service to Baker Street and the City, and linked up with the Tubes and the great Termini of London.

THE Wembley Park Estate Company have erected some shops, each having a self-contained Flat above, in the principal position on the Estate. The price, freehold, of each is £1,600, and possession can be obtained by £200 deposit, balance on easy terms.

Sites are available in excellent positions for the erection of Shops, Flats, and Business Premises. Price from £10 per foot frontage for a minimum of 20 feet frontage. Easy terms of purchase.

The remaining Plots for the erection of Houses or Bungalows can also be purchased on advantageous terms.

Further particulars of H. GIBSON, General Offices, Metropolitan Railway, Baker Street Station, N.W.1.

Telephone: Langham 1130.

"WHERE TO LIVE," illustrating a number of Houses for erection at inclusive prices, can be obtained on application, post free, to The Commercial Manager, Baker Street Station, N.W.1.

Heyday of the Metropolitan in the 1920's – the advertisement for houses is from the 1927 edition of "Metro-Land".

ran during the period of the Exhibition, making a handsome contribution to the Metropolitan's profits.

The LNER opened, in 1924, a short line which diverged from the Marylebone to High Wycombe line near Neasden Junction, with a new station, Wembley Stadium, on a loop, so that trains from London could return there without reversing. During the Exhibition trains ran about every eight minutes, with a journey time of 12 minutes; the fast Metropolitan trains from Baker Street took two minutes less, but as the LNER station was nearer to the Exhibition grounds the convenience of the two train services was about equal. The LNER station was behind the Indian pavilion and was approached through a cutting passing under a replica of old London Bridge. In 1924 these trains were worked by 4-6-2 tanks of Great Central origin but in 1925 five "N7" 0-6-2 tank engines were lent to Neasden ex-GCR shed by Stratford for working the 1925 Exhibition train service. The single-track LNER line was equipped with three-aspect colour-light signalling, which had previously been employed only on the Liverpool Overhead Railway. The Exhibition was also served by LMS and Bakerloo Line trains to Wembley (ex-LNWR) station and by the LNER station at Wembley Hill. The LMSR operated frequent electric trains to Wembley. Special all-day Watford to Broad Street trains augmented the normal timetable and once introduced these exhibition specials continued to run irregularly until September 1929 long after the pageant of Empire had ceased.

Transport within the grounds of the Exhibition was provided by the ''Never-Stop'' Railway, designed by William Yorath Lewis and constructed by "Never-Stop" Transit Ltd., of Kingsway, W.C.2. The cars on this line were kept in constant motion by a revolving shaft laid longitudinally between the rails. Attached to this shaft was a flat bar in the form of a spiral screw; a pair of rollers on each car engaged with the spiral, thus propelling the car. By varying the pitch of the spiral screw, the speed of travel could be varied from 12-16 mph down to 1½-2 mph at stations so that passengers could board and alight without stopping the cars. These, which were 20ft long, ran on rubber-tyred wheels on concrete rails about 8" wide; guide rollers and rails kept the cars on the track. The line, which ran in a south-westerly direction across the Exhibition grounds, consisted of ¾ mile of double track, and cars ran in the same direction all the time, as the two tracks were linked at each end by a semi-circular curve; a special mechanism disengaged the rollers on the car from one spiral shaft and put them into engagement with the other spiral. Power for the electric motors which drove the shafts was generated by the diesel engine from a captured submarine. There were five stations; a covered way connected the North Station with the Metropolitan at Wembley Park, while the South Station was close to the LNER's Wembley Stadium station. The cars, which seated 24 and had standing space, were so arranged that one coach was always in each station. Trains ran from 9 am to 11 pm; fares were 4d (2p) for adults and 2d(1p) for children, and season tickets were available. The line was a great success, and when the Exhibition finally closed on October 19th 1925 its 85 cars had run more than a million miles and carried over two million passengers. Eight of these cars were later sold to the Ashover Light Railway in Derbyshire, opened in April 1925; they were mounted on ex-W.D. bogie wagon frames. A similar "Never-Stop" railway had been opened in the Kursaal Pleasure Gardens at Southend in 1923. The North Station of the Wembley line still survives in industrial use, and several lengths of its concrete superstructure still exist.

Another unusual method of internal transport at the Exhibition was the "Road-Rails" system. The aim of this was to combine in one vehicle the low tractive resistance of rail vehicles with the high adhesion of solid rubber tyres on roads. Just how confident the promoters were of attaining this objective is rather doubtful, because in addition to two

Sentinel steam tractors which each had two rail bogies running on 2ft gauge track and one pair of road wheels, four 4-cylinder Halley tractors were also purchased, and these had two additional road wheels, with only one rail bogie for guiding at the front.. Coaches consisted of semi-open and covered bogie vehicles, each with four compartments. The double-track line ran from the south-west entrance to the Exhibition near Wembley Hill LNER station, to the other terminus some 3,500 ft away at the south side of the Amusement Park, where there was a loop of about 160ft diameter. The system operated in 1924, but it is understood that when the Exhibition reopened for the 1925 season, the "Road-Rails" service was not resumed, as it had not been very successful.

In addition to the foregoing, there were about 200 battery electric cars called 'Railodoks' running on the fifteen or so principal metalled roads within the Exhibition. In total they ran over 150,000 miles and carried 1,000,000 passengers. The 'Railodoks' were used for a variety of ancillary carrying duties – cash in box vans, refuse bins on trailers and fuel oil deliveries in trucks provided with tanks. The 'Railodoks' were manned by the ex-Service Mens' Association and operated on a system very similar to "that brought to perfection by the London General Omnibus Company".

When it was originally conceived in the early 1900s, one of the Exhibition's purposes was be a showcase for resources of British industry and the Empire, at a time when American and German firms were making inroads into the British market. This concept still held good after the Great War, when the Exhibition project was revived. The President of the Board of Trade, Sir Robert Thorne, said in 1920 that the post-war economic boom would soon be over, and trade would sag. We should then be glad of all the trade we could get, and the Exhibition would give a useful boost to British and Empire products.

It was a time of new technology, especially in the field of electricity. Electric domestic appliances were becoming more popular with the modern housewife, and electricity supply was becoming cheaper; labour-saving devices in the home were developing. The country as a whole was, with the exception of the Midlands, in economic decline, but London moved ahead in the consumer boom between the wars, so these new domestic gadgets could be better afforded by London households, and it was a time when house building in the sub-urbs was burgeoning, urged on by the Metropolitan Railway in its "Metro-Land" literature. So, although the Empire Exhibition did little for Britain's economy as a whole, it helped to lay the foundations for London's great manufacturing success between the wars. It was, too, an expression of national confidence and pride in achievement, and there were several examples of progress in industry, architecture and the arts. Medals were awarded for Food of the Empire, Raw Materials, Communications, Machinery and Implements, Manufactures, Homes of the Empire, Education, Science and Art, Recreations, and Traditions of the Empire. The official handbook announced that "Musical and dramatic performances will draw upon talent in the Dominions. Attractions appealing to the young will not be lacking".

Yet in spite of these proud manifestations, the Exhibition was really a last brave flowering of the British Empire, on which the sun was beginning to set. British industrial power, even before the Great War, was waning, and the price paid in that great conflict in men and resources was a heavy one. The larger pavilions, with their Greek classical style, were rather old-fashioned, though the reinforced concrete used to build them was very avant-garde for the mid twenties. Nevertheless, the Exhibition was sufficiently successful to open for a second season in 1925 and must have helped to dispel the feeling of anti-climax which came after the peace celebrations had finished.

A young unemployed ex-First World war airman called Arthur J.Elvin had secured a job as assistant at a cigarette kiosk when the Exhibition opened. He was a young man with great

Wembley Park terminus showing the lavish provision of cars.

View in cutting showing the track and traction arrangement.

Exterior which has changed little since the rebuilding in 1923.

Looking towards Baker Street.

entrepreneurial flair and by the time that the Exhibition closed he had not only married a girl from the adjacent shop but had managed to acquire eight kiosks in the grounds! Elvin then set his sights on the Stadium itself and by shrewd business acumen by 1927 had become first managing director of the new owners, Wembley Stadium Greyhound and Racecourse Ltd. He introduced greyhound racing, speedway racing, Rugby League and other new attractions and of course continued to host the FA Cup Final.

When the exhibition finally closed, several of the temporary pavilions and buildings were dismantled and sold; the Ceylon Pavilion, for instance, became a coachbuilding factory in London, and the Palestine Pavilion a laundry in Glasgow. Others were demolished, but the larger, permanent buildings were left in situ and gradually occupied by industrial firms. Part of the Palace of Industry was sold to the Standard Car Company; some of the land was used for a Country Club with gardens; and the lake was filled in and employed for house building. Several of the larger Exhibition buildings still stood empty in 1927, and "Metro-Land", an attractive booklet issued by the Metropolitan extolling the virtues of that region, said "The vast spaces and terraces of the Exhibition grounds are a place of ghosts".

In 1934 , continuing a policy of expansion, the Wembley Arena was opened as a giant swimming pool which could convert to ice rink or to indoor sports arena.

The 1927 edition of "Metro-Land" was, however, much more optimistic about the prospects of housing development in the Wembley Park area, and claimed "The new Wembley Park is already a popular and populous suburb, and several estate companies are busy on both sides of the railway. These include the Wembley Park Estate and the Chalk Hill Estate which adjoin the line. Another company, which is dealing with a fine triangular site on the southern and eastern slopes of Barn Hill, has recently dispossessed the Wembley Golf Club". Also at Wembley Park ("beautiful open country. One of the healthiest spots around London") were the St. Augustine's Estate, where 3-bedroom houses could be purchased at from £825 to £1,000, and the Kingsbury Hill Estate,"a beautiful residential estate of over 150 acres, amidst charming rural scenery yet less than 6 miles from Marble Arch". A season ticket to Baker Street cost £3-0-9d (£3.04) first class or £2-0-6d (£2.02) second class for three months, local rates were 9s. 8d, (48p) in the pound and rents from £55 to £70 per annum.

The Wembley Park Estate, mentioned above, was built by the Wembley Park Estate Company, successor to the Tower Company; they continued building operations until September 1930, when the firm was voluntarily liquidated, having disposed of all its remaining land and mortgages by then. The estate at Chalk Hill, adjacent to Wembley Park station, was administered by Metropolitan Railway Country Estates Ltd., a railway subsidiary which supervised house building on sites near the line; it had over 120 acres of land and building plots of a quarter of an acre could be bought from £175, with larger sites also available.

All this activity had stimulated considerable goods traffic (this had grown from 2,166 tons in 1914 to over 16,000 tons in 1923), and in November 1923 Selbie, in a letter to the Metropolitan board, urged that the goods yard at Wembley Park should be enlarged, not only to increase accommodation but also to simplify shunting, and he estimated the cost of these works at £3,700, including the transfer of the cart weighbridge from Uxbridge. His plan provided for four new sidings, two 285 ft. long and two 370 ft. long, and a 300 ft. shunting neck.

The delivery of new saloon electric stock in 1921 and of further locomotive-hauled "Dreadnought" compartment coaches two years later put great pressure on the car-sheds at Neasden, and early in 1925 George Hally, the Metropolitan Chief Mechanical Engineer, urged that further accommodation should be provided, as rolling stock was deteriorating through being stored in the open. He wanted the new car-sheds to be built over the Klondike Sidings, between Neasden Works and the running lines, but he was over-ruled by Selbie, the General Manager, in favour of Wembley Park, and on March 25th 1925 the Board authorised the construction of car-sheds capable of housing nine 8-car trains, on the site of the lay-by sidings at the west end of the station. Two ex-War Dept. steel-framed buildings from Credenhill, near Hereford, were purchased from the Perry Barr Metal Co. Ltd., of Birmingham, who undertook to dismantle them, transport them to Wembley Park and re-erect them there, for a total sum of £8,725. Another firm, John Bills of Forest Gate, E.7, laid the foundations. Additional sections were added to the two sheds, making their total length 456 ft. They were brought into use early in 1926, and their existence must have been very beneficial a year later when the new compartment electric trains for the Watford service began to be delivered.

Electric traction had been introduced on the Metropolitan between Baker Street and Harrow, and on the Uxbridge branch, on January 1st 1905. Initially, multiple-unit electric trains provided the train service between Baker Street and Wembley Park and to Uxbridge, with steam trains on the Aylesbury line, but from November 1st 1906 sufficient electric locomotives were available to haul compartment trains of steam stock as far as Wembley Park, where steam engines took them over. In July 1908 the point of change-over from electric to steam power was moved to Harrow, but the exchange of motive power was still occasionally made at Wembley Park until electric traction was extended to Rickmansworth on January 1st 1925.

During the Hitler War the Stadium was a venue for many fund-raising charitable events and was used as a temporary camp for thousands of weary soldiers brought back from the beaches of Dunkirk. In July 1948 the first post-war Olympic Games, the XIV Olympiad, were held at the Stadium with massive and indispensable financial support from the owning company.

Wembley Park station was partially rebuilt to cater for the extra traffic generated by the Games; a second entrance, booking hall and passenger overbridge were provided.

At the beginning of the 1960's the Wembley Complex became part of the British Electric Traction group of companies, and in 1977 saw the opening of the Wembley Conference Centre. Meantime on September 1st 1969 British Railways had closed Wembley Stadium station and the Neasden North Junction loop. (The last train to use the Stadium station brought supporters to the Rugby League Cup Final on May 18th 1968.)

Prompted by the opening of the Conference Centre, British Railways changed the name of neglected Wembley Hill on 8th May 1978 to Wembley Complex and the next day Sir Henry Marking, Chairman of the British Tourist Authority visited to unveil the new name-boards subtitled "for Wembley Conference Centre, Stadium and Arena." ' A revised service of 9 down and 12 up trains on Mondays to Fridays was provided initially.

The Stanmore Branch

The final developments affecting Wembley Park before the Metropolitan Railway was absorbed by the London Passenger Transport Board in 1933 were the quadrupling of the tracks between Wembley Park and Harrow-on-the-Hill, and the opening of the branch from the former station to Stanmore. These works were both authorised by the Metropolitan Railway Development Act, 1930. The track quadrupling, with the new tracks on the up side of the line, was completed on November 22nd 1931.

In view of the fact that severe congestion was already being caused by the bottle-neck between Finchley Road and Baker Street, where there were only two tracks in tunnel, it is

LONDON TRANSPORT MUSEUM

Stanmore train composed of "MV" stock entering Wembley Park station, circa 1933. The Metropolitan power station at Neasden can be seen in the Background and the special platform for Exhibition traffic is on the left.

LCGB KEN NUNN COLLECTION

"Railway World" Special passing Wembley Park en route for Stanmore hauled by No. 1 "John Lyon"
22nd May, 1955.

rather surprising that the Met. should contemplate, as late as 1930, building yet another suburban branch and further adding to the number of trains passing over these two tracks. But financial help for public works which would help to create employment was available from the Government under the Development (Loan Guarantees and Grants) Act, 1929, and the Metropolitan board decided to seize this opportunity for one last act of expansion while they were still independent. They applied successfully for a grant under the Development Act, and on November 20th 1930 a contract was signed for the construction of the branch by Walter, Scott & Middleton Ltd., of Westminster, at a cost of £168,628, The new line left the main line about ½ mile north of Wembley Park, with intermediate stations at Kingsbury and Canons Park Edgware, and a terminus at Stanmore, about 4½ miles from Wembley Park. It had been hoped to open the new line in the autumn of 1932, but difficulties in obtaining possession of some of the land, and very wet weather in the summer of 1931 which made the heavy Middlesex clay difficult to handle, caused delays, and the line was not opened until December 10th 1932.

Some heavy engineering works were involved in construction, including the excavation of 470,000 yards of soil, seven bridges, and the diversion of the Wealdstone Brook near the junction with the main line. The signalling with automatic 3-aspect colour-lights and train stops, was the first example of centralised traffic control anywhere outside America, all the points and signals on the branch being controlled from a new signal box at Wembley Park. The stations at Stanmore and Kingsbury were designed by C.W. Clark, the Metropolitan's architect, and are in a restrained but pleasing domestic villa style. Canons Park Edgware ("Edgware" was later dropped from the title) has its platforms on a six-arch viaduct, and a steel girder bridge carries the railway over Whitchurch Lane. A further station, Queensbury, was opened, originally as a halt, between Kingsbury and Canons Park on December 16th 1934. Extensive housing development in the district led to a spacious entrance hall being added by London Transport in 1936, and the platform shelters were rebuilt fourteen years later.

The ceremonial opening of the line took place on December 9th 1932, and was on a lavish scale; the Metropolitan, always a publicity-conscious company and aware that within little over six months it would lose its identity in the new London Passenger Transport Board, obviously wanted to make this, their swan song, a really memorable occasion. The special train consisted of two 1930 "MW" stock compartment motor coaches, three first class compartment trailers, the Rothschild saloon and the Pullman car "Mayflower". This would have entailed fitting the latter two vehicles with buckeye couplings, and with power and control cables so that they could run in a multiple-unit train. On board were the Minister of Transport P.J.Pybus, the Metropolitan chairman (Lord Aberconway) and other officers, in addition to dignitaries of other railways and members of the Press. At Wembley Park the party inspected the new signal box, and the Minister opened the branch by operating a switch which energised all the signals and points. Much was made in publicity of this remote control aspect, and the ceremony was even filmed by British Movietone News. After travelling over the branch and inspecting the new stations, the party travelled back to Baker Street, where luncheon for 194 guests was served in Chiltern Hall, part of the large block of flats erected over Baker Street Station.

The public opening was the following day, December 10th, and a lavish service of 144 trains a day was provided, with the first "shuttle" train leaving Stanmore for Wembley Park at 5.14 am, and the first through train to Baker Street departing at 5.35 am. Some of the Baker Street trains, after stopping at Canons Park and Kingsbury called only at Neasden and Dollis Hill, reaching Baker Street in 25 minutes, as against 31 minutes for the slow trains. In addition, there was a frequent "shuttle" service between Stanmore and Wembley Park, worked by one of the two composite compartment motor coaches equipped with driving compartments at both ends so that they could work as single units. There were, however, no through trains to the City, possibly because of peak hour congestion on the Inner Circle, so passengers for destinations east of Baker Street had to change trains there.

In its new timetable published on December 10th the Metropolitan announced that "Two years of strenuous labour coupled with an expenditure of over half a million pounds, has resulted in hitherto inaccessible countryside, offering unlimited scope for building operations, being brought into close touch with town, and thus providing London with a much needed outlet for its ever increasing population." It would "provide room, under healthy, happy conditions, for a considerable population, while the pleasant lanes, meadow tracks and by-ways that abound in the district will also soon become popular with pleasure seekers". This is typical of the Metro-Land literature published by the company's enterprising Publicity Department; great play was made with rural-sounding names like Uxendon Farm and Honeypot Lane, and the piece stated that "past experience makes it safe to anticipate a steady stream of migration from the congested areas of the Metropolis in a short space of time". It has always seemed to me very ironic that these blandishments to Londoners to move out into the fields and woods of rural arcadia inevitably resulted in these unspoilt country districts becoming covered with bricks and mortar, though admittedly a home in Metro-Land was certainly preferable to the smoky congestion of central London.

On July 1st 1933 the Metropolitan Railway was absorbed by the London Passenger Transport Board; at first, this brought little change to the Stanmore branch. But later it was to figure in a scheme to obviate the congestion caused, as has already been mentioned, by the bottle-neck between Finchley Road and Baker Street, where there were only two tracks, in tunnel. To have widened the existing lines with new tunnels would have been very costly; the Metropolitan considered several schemes to solve this problem, including a deep level tube from Kilburn to Edgware Road, but because of the expense involved none of these came to fruition. But in 1935 financial assistance was available from the Government, and it was decided to build a new tube railway, just over two miles in length, from the Bakerloo Line at Baker Street, coming to the surface at Finchley Road, where interchange with Metropolitan Line trains would be possible. Bakerloo Line trains would be extended over the Metropolitan branch to Stanmore. Work began in 1936; the Metropolitan Line tracks between Finchley Road and Wembley Park were rearranged so that Bakerloo Line trains could use the two inner lines, leaving the two outer tracks for fast Metropolitan Line trains. To avoid Bakerloo Line trains having to cross on the level the up Metropolitan line, a burrowing junction was built just north of Wembley Park. The Metropolitan stations at Lords, Marlborough Road and Swiss Cottage were closed, and new deep level stations on the Bakerloo Line were built at Swiss Cottage and St. John's Wood to replace them.

Work on this scheme was well in hand when war broke out on September 3rd 1939, so the work was completed, and a service of Bakerloo Line trains between Stanmore and Elephant & Castle was introduced on November 20th, 1939, with a maximum of seven trains an hour on the Stanmore line section.

Further changes were in store for the Stanmore line. In the London Plan Working Party Report of 1949 a new tube, the Fleet Line, was projected. This was to take over the Bakerloo Line tracks between Stanmore and Baker Street, run in new tube tunnels to Charing Cross, and then continue to Fenchurch Street and Surrey Docks to join the East London Line and serve New Cross, with a possible extension to Lewisham. Later proposals envisaged taking the new line along beneath the Thames to the Dockland area.

Work began on the Baker Street to Charing Cross section in 1972; this involved separate tube tunnels for the Bakerloo and Jubilee lines, whereas hitherto Bakerloo trains from Queens Park and from Stanmore had shared the same tubes. In 1977 the name of the new railway was changed to Jubilee Line. New stations were opened at Baker Street, Bond Street (giving interchange facilities with the Central Line), and Green Park (interchange with the Victoria and Piccadilly Lines), while at Charing Cross a new station served the Jubilee Line and also incorporated the former Strand (Northern Line) and Trafalgar Square (Bakerloo Line) stations. The Jubilee Line was officially opened on April 30th 1979 by the Prince of Wales; he travelled the length of the line to Stanmore, riding in the driving cab of the inaugural train, which was composed of 1972 Mark II stock, for most of the journey.

To return to Wembley Park station itself, this was partially rebuilt in 1948 to cater for extra traffic generated by the Olympic Games, which were held in the Stadium; a second entrance, booking hall and passenger overbridge were provided. Six years later the track layout and signalling were altered, to provide six platform roads. Fast and slow Metropolitan Line trains in both directions keep to separate paths from the east end of the station as far as Harrow; Jubilee Line trains also have their own lines, together with an independent reversal neck between the east and westbound tracks just west of the station platform, The original Exhibition platform of 1923 has disappeared, probably during the alterations just mentioned, but the buildings at street level are little changed.

Plans are now in hand for the complete rebuilding of Wembley Park station; these include a new commuter ticket hall, a separate stadium ticket hall over the car park, a new glass canopy over the whole station, with a vertical beacon to act as a local landmark. These works are scheduled for completion in March 1998, to tie in with the opening of the Jubilee Line Extension to Greenwich and Stratford.

This concludes the story of the Metropolitan at Wembley Park, a history which has seen far-reaching changes, from the simple two-platform station of 1893, its enlargement the following year to cater for Watkin's ill-fated Tower, its further rebuilding during the heady days of the British Empire Exhibition, to the Bakerloo and Jubilee Line changes of 1939 and forty years later. What began as an unimportant wayside station is now one of the busiest on the Metropolitan Line. But the Stadium, the largest edifice built for the Empire Exhibition, is, happily, still in constant use, and so are some of the other buildings; the Palace of Engineering, occupied by a firm of carpet merchants, the Palace of Industry, used by the Stadium as a store, and the Fiji Pavilion, which, much extended, survives in industrial use. Traces of the Never-Stop Railway terminus can still be seen in North End Road near Wembley Park station, and sections of its concrete superstructure still survive. There is even one relic of Watkin's Tower, in the shape of the manager's house, now No. 85 Wembley Park Drive, on the corner of Oakington Avenue. Also worth mentioning is the former Met sports ground, a 13-acre site at Forty Lane, Wembley Park. This included an army recreational hut built, with the aid of a loan from the Metropolitan, from a war memorial fund raised among the staff in 1919. Lectures, ambulance training, educational classes and entertainments were held here from 1922, and the annual sports meetings were attended by the chairman, vice-chairman and general manager, to present the prizes and encourage the staff. The "Remembrance Hall" was destroyed by fire in 1929, and a London Regional Transport home for retired staff now occupies the site.

There are pleasant reminders, too, of the old Metropolitan Railway in the stations at Kingsbury and Stanmore and the street level building at Wembley Park station, links with those expansionist days of Metro-Land, when cinemas, shopping parades and semi-detached houses with half-timbering and stained glass windows were spreading across the Middlesex fields.

The freight traffic, however, is a thing of the past, the goods yard having been converted to a car park in October 1966.

First Wembley Cup Final – Bolton Wanderers v West Ham – April 28th 1923. In the background the Loop Line, all around green fields and on the pitch thousands, and thousands more streaming to get in.

The Great Central Northolt to Neasden Line

In competing for passenger traffic between London and Birmingham the Great Western Railway was for many years at a disadvantage, as the rival London & North Western route was much shorter. The Great Central, which had opened its London Extension in 1899 by joining up with the Metropolitan at Quainton Road, north of Aylesbury, thus gaining access over Met. metals to their new terminus at Marylebone, was having problems with working its express trains over the congested and heavily graded Metropolitan route. These were exacerbated by strained relations between William Politt, the Great Central general manager, and John Bell, his counterpart on the Metropolitan. As a result, the two companies got together and in August 1899 the Great Western & Great Central Joint Committee was set up.

The GWR opened a new line from Acton to High Wycombe early in 1905. This linked up with the existing line from High Wycombe to Princes Risborough. A further stage was the opening, on November 20th 1905, of a line from Princes Risborough to Ashendon Junction, the first section of a new direct route through the Chilterns to Birmingham, bypassing Oxford completely. Finally, this line was extended from Ashendon Junction to Aynho Junction, just south of Banbury. Opened in 1910, this gave the Great Western a much shorter route to Birmingham (110 miles compared with 129 miles by the old route), and brought that city within two hours journey time from Paddington, putting them on equal terms with the LNWR.

The section of the new route between Northolt and Ashendon Junction was handed over to the Great Western & Great Central Joint Committee, and the GCR built a line running northwards from Ashendon Junction to Grendon Underwood Junction, a few miles north of Quainton Road, where it joined the original Great Central route from Rugby and the north.

By this means the Great Central had a much easier and less congested line into London, though 4½ miles longer it was much easier to operate, and also offered a share in suburban traffic from stations on the joint line between Northolt and High Wycombe. All that remained was for the Great Central to build a link from the GW & GC joint line at Northolt to Neasden, where their trains would rejoin their original Metropolitan & GC Joint route into London. It is with this short line that we are particularly concerned here, as it passes through the Wembley area.

The GW & GC Joint line between Northolt and Ashendon Junction opened to freight traffic on November 20th 1905 and to passenger trains on March 1st 1906, with local services to Paddington and Marylebone and Great Central expresses via Grendon Underwood. The line from Northolt Junction to Neasden South Junction, 6 miles 30 chains long, was authorised by Act of Parliament on August 12th 1898, and the contract for building it was awarded to Thomas Oliver & Sons of Rugby at a price of £197,955. In December 1902 the GCR Engineer, C.A. Rowlandson, reported that very good progress was being made; about a third of the earthworks were completed, and work on the bridge over the LNWR at Sudbury, and the covered way under the District Ealing & South Harrow line (itself under construction at that time) was in hand. The line was opened for coal and goods traffic on November 20th 1905 and to passengers on March 1st 1906.

It transpired that the construction costs were much higher than anticipated, due to several factors; the earthworks along the line were very treacherous, and slopes of cuttings had to be 1 in 3 instead of 1 in 2 as originally specified in the contract. Abnormally heavy rainfall in 1903 had resulted in embankments settling, in one case from 30 ft high to only 15 ft, necessitating piledriving and a heavy retaining wall. Drainage on cuttings cost an extra £2,202, and bridges had to have larger foundations owing to the softness of the ground. Four tracks instead of two had been laid between Blind Lane and Brent Bridge, Neasden. All these extra works resulted in a total construction cost of £341,835, plus permanent way costing £32,071, provided by the Great Central but laid by the contractor. Intermediate stations at Wembley Hill and at Sudbury & Harrow Road were built by Pattinson & Son for £3,951 and £4,617 respectively, and at South Harrow & Roxeth by Moss & Son at a cost of £3,688. Signalling was provided by Saxby & Farmer at a cost of £6,515.

As already mentioned, there were four tracks between Brent Bridge, Neasden and Blind Lane (close to where the LNWR main line was crossed by a lattice girder bridge), with the fast tracks in the centre and local lines on the outside. The stations at Wembley Hill, Sudbury & Harrow Road and at South Harrow all had loops to the up and down main lines with the platforms outside, so that the anticipated frequent local trains could use these loops to pick up passengers, while main line trains passed through on the fast lines in the centre.

Local passenger traffic was, however, slow to build up, as the country was still rural. So the original Marylebone to South Harrow shuttle service was provided by a steam rail-motor; the carriage portion of this had first and third class saloons divided by a passenger entrance protected by collapsible gates, while steps gave access from rail level. At the front end, instead of the usual bogie, was a small 0-4-0 tank engine, with horizontal boiler and the chimney protruding through the roof. At the rear of the 61' 6" body was a driving compartment. An unusually modern feature for this time was electric lighting. Many railways adopted the steam rail-motor during this period, often to counter competition from electric tramways, which were burgeoning during the early 1900s. In the Great Central's case, however, the rail-motor was introduced in anticipation of tramcar competition; the Metropolitan Electric Tramways Company was building its Route 62 from Paddington Green to Elton Avenue, Sudbury, close to Sudbury & Harrow Road station – the route was opened in 1910.

After some time problems arose with the riding of the rail-motor car, which developed an unpleasant motion, and it was taken off the South Harrow service. So late in 1906 the rail-car was replaced by three small Sacré 2-4-0 tank engines hauling large 12-wheeled carriages which had a driving compartment at one end, with a steam regulator, reversing lever and whistle. When driving from this compartment the driver could communicate with the fireman, who remained on the footplate of the locomotive, by means of a whistle code when, for instance, the brakes needed to he applied.

Traffic did start to build up, and in 1908 the "push-and-pull" set was replaced on the South Harrow service by an ordinary train; a photograph of this period shows a Robinson 4-4-2 tank engine and three compartment bogie coaches at South Harrow. But Sam Fay, the GCR's enterprising General Manager, was a great believer in railcars as a way of countering tramway competition, and on March 28th 1912 a new petrol-electric vehicle was given a press run to South Harrow and back. It was built by the United Car Company of Preston, famous as builders of tramcars, and was 41' 6" long with a teak body. Inside it consisted of a driving cab, equipped for one-man operation, a compartment containing a 90hp 6-cylinder engine driving a dynamo coupled to two British Westinghouse electric motors, a third class saloon on either side of a central entrance, and a driving compartment with provision for

Steam Navvy toils in Wembley cutting during construction of the Neasden-Northolt line of the GCR, 1902.

MILEPOST 92½ COLLECTION

Special hauled by 2-6-0 No. 1635 still in GNR colours passes beneath the Stadium wall with a veteran mixed rake behind.

*"N7" 0-6-2T 997E
approaching Stadium station
4th July, 1925.*

H. C. CASSERLEY

*2-6-4T "L3" 69061 on
football special on loop,
circa 1949.*

C. R. L. COLES

*In latter days the Stadium
platform slumbers in austere
loneliness.*

FRANK GOUDIE

50

Norway cruise boat train for Immingham Dock passing in 1938 hauled by "Lord Faringdon" type "B3" 4-6-0 No. 6167

luggage. Accommodation was for 50 in the throw-over rattan seats popular in tramcars at that time.

The trial run was very successful; the press were impressed by the vehicle's absence of vibration, even when starting and at speed, and the senior Great Central officers were also very enthusiastic. It went into regular service on the South Harrow line, though for how long is rather uncertain. However, it seems probable that as traffic developed the petrol-electric car, even hauling a six-wheeled coach, became incapable of handling the loads. So it was replaced by steam trains, hauled at first by Robinson 4-4-2 tank locomotives (LNER Class "C13"), later succeeded by the same designer's 4-6-2 tanks (LNER Class "A5") which headed trains composed of the handsome matchboard-panelled coaches which Robinson built for the Marylebone services. Three Marylebone to Manchester expresses were switched to the GW & GC Joint route in 1906, and these gradually increased in number, hauled by Robinson 4-4-0s (LNER Class "D9") and later by the famous "Director" class 4-4-0 which appeared from 1913 onwards. Examples of the several types of 4-6-0 built by Robinson also appeared, including, in the 1930s, "Sir. Sam Fay" (Class "B2") and "Lord Faringdon" (Class "B3") machines, which, among other services, hauled the Norway Cruise Boat Trains to Immingham, from whence the fortunate and wealthy were taken for cruises along the coast of Norway.

Northolt Junction was without a station until July 1908, when the station there, jointly owned by the Great Western and the Great Central, was opened; renamed South Ruislip & Northolt Junction in 1932, it became simply "South Ruislip" fifteen years later. Although the cutting at Wembley Hill had been lined with a retaining wall 30ft high and 158 ft long, the unstable clay soil caused a major landslip there in February 1918. Cracks developed in the wall in several places, and the tracks were distorted into strange shapes. The train service was held up for two weeks, and Great Central services via High Wycombe were re-routed over the GWR into Paddington. Rectifying this earthslip involved new retaining walls, concrete struts, draining and flattening the cutting slopes, temporary tracks and diverting the main line, at a total cost of £84,112.

Automatic three-aspect colour signalling was introduced between Marylebone (Goods Box) and Neasden South Junction in October 1922; the contractors for this were the Westlinghouse Brake & Saxby Signal Co. at a cost of £5,853, the Great Central dealing with the running and fixing of wires themselves.

In 1921 plans for the British Empire Exhibition at Wembley were announced, and the Great Central hoped for a good share of the extra passenger traffic which this would generate, as the Exhibition grounds were very near to their station at Wembley Hill; journey time from Marylebone was 12 minutes, the same as that from Baker Street to Wembley Park on the Metropolitan. It appears that at first Wembley Hill station was considered adequate for the Exhibition traffic, but on November 10th, 1921, the GCR Board authorised the construction of a loop line, which left the Neasden - Northolt line just west of Neasden South Junction and ran right around the Exhibition site, with a special Wembley Stadium station to serve the Exhibition . When the LNER, successors to the Great Central, began building this station on the loop the Metropolitan objected, saying that it went against the spirit of the Metropolitan & Great Central Joint Committee agreement that the GCR should not convey local traffic between Marylebone and Harrow. The LNER replied that, as the loop was connected to the Neasden-Northolt line and not under the jurisdiction of the Joint Committee, this agreement did not apply. Both companies took legal advice, the Metropolitan being informed that it had no case.

In the meantime, Wembley Stadium was built and completed in time for for the Cup Final between Bolton Wanderers and West Ham to be played there on April 28th 1923. As already noted, huge crowds attended (there were 19 main line trains from the north and eventually trains were standing nose to tail on the main line). The inadequacy of the new Stadium station on the Loop line to cope with crowds like this was apparent (it consisted simply of one long platform, without a canopy). So the LNER (which had absorbed the Great Central on January 1st 1923) authorised, at its Board meeting on February 1st 1924 some radical improvements, including a decorative concrete screen, an awning 290 ft long and 15 ft wide, seating accommodation, and booking offices at both ends of the platform. Trains from Marylebone could call at the new station, which was renamed "Exhibition", and then continue around the loop line and back to London without reversing; this and the new automatic colour-light signalling made it possible to run trains at three minutes head-way. The Exhibition station was designed to handle 16,000 passengers an hour, and it was in use in time for the opening of the British Empire Exhibition in April 1924.

In 1921 the British Empire Exhibition authorities had written to Lord Faringdon, the GCR Chairman, asking for a contribution to the Exhibition's capital, but Lord Faringdon refused, saying the Great Central had no powers to subscribe. In January 1922 the GCR agreed to construct a siding at Wembley for the Exhibition's use; the cost of this, estimated at £3,000, to be borne by the Exhibition authorities. In September of that year the Great Central Board authorised the provision of two new hoardings at Wembley Hill station, to publicise their services to the Exhibition. The Exhibition was very popular; it closed in October 1924 but reopened the following year from April to October. In all nearly 27,000,000 people passed through its turnstiles. This heavy traffic was of great benefit to the LNER, whose train service from Marylebone was handled expeditiously by ex-GCR "A5" 4-6-2 tank engines and a number of ex-Great Eastern "N7" 0-6-2Ts which were transferred from Stratford for the purpose.

After the Exhibition closed, the Stadium station and loop continued to be used by special trains catering for spectators at the Cup Final, which continued to be played at Wembley, and other sporting events, including the 1948 Olympic Games, until September 1st 1969, when the facilities were closed; the last train was a Rugby League special on May 18th 1968. Wembley Hill station was renamed Wembley Complex from May 9th 1978, at a ceremony performed by the chairman of the British Tourist Authority. It now boasted a service of 12 up and 9 down trains daily. It has recently been given the more logical title of Wembley Stadium.

When the Neasden - Northolt line was opened, much of the area through which it passed was open country, but housing development soon began. Ruislip-Northwood Urban District Council produced in 1909 an ambitious plan for a Garden City, whose "Victoria Avenue" would run from Northolt southwards to Northolt Junction. Between Sudbury Hill, Harrow (which was then named South Harrow) and the District Railway's Sudbury station, two roads of terrace houses, Rosebank Avenue and Fernbank Avenue, were built in 1910/15; residents there would have enjoyed good facilities for travel to central London, as these two stations are only a short distance apart. In the 1920s Homefield Road and Priory Road were built near Sudbury & Harrow Road station by the British Freehold Investment Company. The coming of the British Empire Exhibition to Wembley in 1924/25 made people aware of the attractions of the area, giving a considerable boost to housing development and to some light industry; these gradually began to cover the open fields around Wembley Hill, Sudbury & Harrow Road and Sudbury Hill stations.

In the late 1920s and 1930s locally passenger trains were usually of five bogie coaches, though some Gresley articulated twin sets were introduced in 1930; usually ex-GCR "A5"

4-6-2 tanks provided the motive power. In the summer of 1949 a service of push-pull trains appeared, consisting of two Gresley coaches hauled by an ex-Great Eastern "N7" 0-6-2T. Nationalisation, however, brought changes, when 35 Thompson "L1" 2-6-4 tanks went to Neasden shed by Summer 1950. The Robinson "A5" 4-6-2 tanks still lingered a little longer, as "L1s" were prohibited from working over the Princes Risborough - Aylesbury line. Later the former GCR lines were handed over from Eastern to the London Midland Region, and LMS type 2-6-4 tank engines replaced the "L1s".

More exalted trains did traverse the line, of course, such as the "Master Cutler" (Marylebone to Sheffield), which sometimes boasted an "A3" Pacific, and the "South Yorkshireman", headed by a "V2" 2-6-2. The "Starlight Special" cheap-fare overnight trains to Scotland, introduced in the early 1950s, were also routed this way.

Full diesel operation of suburban services to Marylebone began on June 18th 1962, with a new timetable, under which an hourly interval service came into force between West Ruislip and Marylebone, calling at South Ruislip, Northolt Park, Sudbury Hill, Sudbury & Harrow Road, and Wembley Hill. Previously only a number of peak-hour trains had called at these intermediate stations. The new 4-car diesel units were built at Derby with British United Traction engines totalling 920 hp.

In 1970 it was announced that the line would be closed, as the Minister of Transport considered that better value for money was likely by the return of the High Wycombe service to Paddington, but fortunately this never happened. The current train service, worked by Class 165 "Turbo" diesel multiple-units since 1991/2, is basically to High Wycombe and Princes Risborough, with some trains extended to Leamington Spa or the reopened Birmingham (Snow Hill). All stations are unmanned, and trains call at Sudbury & Harrow Road and at Sudbury Hill, Harrow only in the peak hours, For six weeks in October and November 1967 the Paddington-Birmingham service was diverted to Marylebone during the resignalling of Paddington station, and this brought Western Region "Warship" Class diesel locomotives to the line. Other Western Region locomotives to appear on the line included ex-GWR "61XX" 2-6-2 tanks, when the route was transferred to the WR and they were used on local passenger trains.

The only stations catering for freight traffic were Sudbury Hill, and Sudbury & Harrow Road; both had 5-ton cranes. The former was able to handle livestock traffic, but unlike Sudbury & Harrow Road it could not cope with "furniture vans, carriages, portable engines and machines on wheels", to quote the Railway Clearing House handbook of stations. Business was mainly of coal and package traffic, and motive power consisted of ex-Great Central "J11" 0-6-0s, replaced from 1954 by B.R. Standard Class "4" 2-6-0s. In the final days of the local goods trains a Class "27" diesel locomotive put in an appearance.

Freight services were withdrawn during the Beeching cuts, but they have recently made a come-back in the shape of private sidings at the north end of the line near Neasden South Junction. One of these serves a large new factory for T.P. Dibdin & Co., built over the former carriage sidings. I have been unable to establish what products are manufactured here, but there is evidently a considerable export trade, as large numbers of Continental vans appear in the sidings, and are moved around by a small diesel shunter. The other sidings belong to Balfour Beatty Ltd. who have contracts for renewing permanent way for British Rail, for which purpose they receive ARC/Yeomans stone trains which deliver ballast.

Today the line is a shadow of its former self, and there is sadly little to remind one of the old Great Central Railway. The original stations, which were of a rather attractive GCR standard design in brick with wide wooden platform canopies, have all been completely

LENS OF SUTTON

C. R. L. COLES

Up goods hauled by ROD 2-8-0, circa 1938.

rebuilt; the platforms at Sudbury & Harrow Road were originally of timber, but deteriorated to the point of being dangerous, so they were replaced by an island platform and a tiny shelter at the top of the steps leading up from road level. Sudbury Hill, Harrow station has up and down platforms where the former loops used to be; each has a small brick and concrete shelter. The only trace of the old station is a cast-iron milepost on the up platform, and even this has been resited. Northolt Park has a corrugated iron shelter, and at South Ruislip there are two platforms with one central track; the down line from Neasden passes under the Western Region/LT Central Line tracks by an underpass. The Great Western station (formerly Northolt Junction) was completely rebuilt in London Transport Holden style and renamed South Ruislip in 1947, when the Central Line was extended to West Ruislip.

So the Neasden - Northolt line, which once boasted comfortable stations, frequent trains, through named expresses and even a boat train, now has intermediate stations which are virtually unmanned halts and only used for peak-hour trains. However, the new Class 165 "Turbo" DMUs are fast and quite comfortable, and some even have a trolley refreshment service, so some aspects of the line's amenities have improved.

Stations names have been changed several times, so the following chart may prove helpful :-

Original Name	New Name	
Wembley Hill	Wembley Complex (1978)	Wembley Stadium (1991)
South Harrow & Roxeth	Sudbury Hill, Harrow (1926)	
Sudbury & Harrow Road	Unchanged	
Northolt Park for Northolt Village (opened 1926)	Northolt Park	
Northolt Junction	South Ruislip & Northolt Junction (12/9/1932)	South Ruislip (30/6/1947)

The original Wembley Stadium station on the loop line was closed on 1st September, 1969

ALPERTON

District
and Piccadilly

The Piccadilly Line of London Transport passes through the borough of Wembley, from a point between Alperton and Park Royal stations, to just short of Sudbury Hill. This began life as the Ealing & South Harrow Railway, incorporated by an Act of 25 August 1894, with a working agreement with the District Railway. A contract with C. J. Wills was signed in November 1897; work on the new line began two months later, and the track was all laid by the end of 1899. Matters then hung fire for a while, but the Directors of the District reported in June 1902 that "the line is now being prepared for electric traction and it is hoped will be open by the end of the year". The short section from Ealing (Hanger Lane Junction) to Park Royal was opened on 25th June 1903, to serve the Royal Agricultural Society's Show at Park Royal, becoming the first section of the District to be worked permanently by electric traction; three days later services were extended to South Harrow. Current was taken from a temporary generating station at Alperton until Lots Road power station came into use on 1st February 1905, and the service was operated originally by two seven-car trains of District Railway "A" Stock, of decidedly American appearance, with clerestories and gated open end balconies, in addition to double sliding doors in the centre of each car. Some trains were still steam hauled until the end of December 1905, when electric traction took over completely. Travellers to the West End and City changed into steam trains at Mill Hill Park – now Acton Town – until 1905.

In the meantime, the District had promoted a Bill for the Harrow, Uxbridge & High Wycombe Railway which was to extend through Beaconsfield to High Wycombe. This came up for consideration by Parliament on 11th March 1897, but the people of High Wycombe, who had initially given their support, lost interest, perhaps because they knew of the projected Great Western & Great Central Joint Railway which would pass through their town. So the High Wycombe section, which was opposed by the GWR, was refused. But Railway No.1, a line 6½ miles long between South Harrow & Uxbridge, was sanctioned as the Harrow & Uxbridge Railway, with a working agreement with the District company included. The amended Bill duly received the Royal Assent, but the District, who had already overstretched their resources in building the Ealing & South Harrow line and the Whitechapel & Bow Railway, were unable to proceed with construction.

As a result, the people of Uxbridge, who had looked to the District for a more convenient rail connection to London than the Great Western branch from West Drayton, were driven into the arms of the Metropolitan, whose Extension Line passed through Harrow-on-the-Hill, only about two miles from the Ealing & South Harrow's projected terminus at South Harrow.

The Met's directors quickly seized this opportunity to beat their old rivals the District, and as a result it was they who built the new railway into Uxbridge, which ran from Harrow-on-the-Hill and through Rayners Lane, from whence a spur connected with the District station at South Harrow. After the usual contention between the Met and the District, the latter's trains did finally reach Uxbridge from 1st March 1910 over this spur, which was never used by a regular Metropolitan passenger service. The Harrow & Uxbridge's agreement with the District Railway had been cancelled in favour of one with the Metropolitan, and the line was opened on July 4th 1904, with steam traction until January 1st 1905, when the new power Station at Neasden was ready and electric traction came into use.

Stations on the Ealing & South Harrow line were opened at North Ealing, Park Royal & Twyford Abbey (closed in 1931 in favour of a new station at Park Royal some distance to the south (this was named Park Royal (Hanger Hill) from 1936 to 1947), Alperton (named Perivale-Alperton until 1910), Sudbury Town, Sudbury Hill, and South Harrow. The original South Harrow station was closed in 1935 when a new station was opened a short distance to the north. The Metropolitan had opened a halt at Rayners Lane, at that time a very rural place, in 1906 and, as already noted District trains reached this, and thence the Uxbridge line, from March 1st 1910. The District's Ealing Common to Uxbridge service was handed over to the Piccadilly Line in two stages, Ealing Common to South Harrow on July 4th 1932, and thence to Uxbridge on October 23rd 1933, and trains of "Standard" tube stock took the place of the very mixed formations which the District Line had provided.

The Ealing & South Harrow line was one of the earliest Underground Group railways to see the burgeoning of the new style of architecture introduced by Charles Holden, when Sudbury Town was rebuilt as a prototype for future developments. Opened in 1931, it is widely regarded as an outstanding example of 1930s railway architecture, and was one of the very first thirties buildings to achieve "listed" status, hence the survival there of the now redundant passimeter booking office. The station building is a brick boxlike structure with a flat concrete roof; two main entrances are surmounted by vertical windows which extend up to the roof, which is high and makes for a spacious concourse. Platform canopies, in ferro-concrete, are cantilevered out from the station buildings, and it was part of Holden's philosophy that all the station's details should harmonise its modern design; subway entrances, light fittings, platform seats and station signs and symbols. The effect of the main station building is plain, dignified and rather austere, and Sudbury Town became the forerunner of many similar station rebuildings, including those at Alperton, Sudbury Hill, and the new, re-sited station at South Harrow. After Park Royal was rebuilt in 1936, the only station on the Ealing & South Harrow line in original condition was North Ealing, and this still remains very much like a country station, with its wooden canopies and iron footbridge. Incidentally, an interesting point about the district of Sudbury is that it saw electric trains before steam trains; the District Railway arriving in 1903, before the Great Central with its steam service began operations at Sudbury & Harrow Road and Sudbury Hill three years later.

Housing development along the South Harrow line was slow at first, and came only gradually, with long rows of new terraced houses at Northolt Park; as residents here and at Whitton Avenue in Sudbury found it more convenient to catch a bus to the District at Sudbury Hill rather than the slower steam trains from the Great Central stations at Sudbury Hill, Harrow and Sudbury & Harrow Road. At the Northern end of the District line housing was later in coming but, once started, it soon accelerated; in the 1930s the Depression resulted in many builders from the north of England descending on the metropolis, and the fields and woods surrounding London were soon covered with "Tudorbethan" semi-detached housing and shopping areas. In the words of Dennis Edwards "they finally achieved complete ruin of the landscape from the LNER Marylebone line at Field End Road to the shops at South Harrow". Housing development was encouraged in those days, but now, when TV aerials, and even TV satellite dishes, decorate the houses, this heavy commuter traffic is more of an embarrassment than a blessing to train operators.

Some notes on the different types of rolling stock used on the line may be of interest. When it opened in 1903 the service, the first District Railway electrification, using the

58

Traditional clean lines of London Transport – Cockfosters train at Sudbury Town station, Autumn 1995.

District Railway "B" stock train near Sudbury Hill station in 1905. Work on the construction of the Great Central station can be seen in the background.

550 volt d,c, system, was operated by trains of "A" stock, two 7-car trains of which were built by the Brush Electrical Engineering Co. Ltd. of Loughborough to an American design. The two end motor-cars in each train had half-cabs in luggage compartments at one end and gated platforms at the other. Trailers had gated platforms at both ends; the intermediate motor cars had fold-up driving positions on the gate platforms. All cars had double sliding doors in the centre of each side. They were at first painted bright yellow with maroon lining, but by 1905 they received the red livery used on District main line stock.

From 1905 until the line was handed over to the Piccadilly Line in 1932/33 trains consisted of various classes of District stock, from Class "B" wooden cars through to Class "L" of 1931; with the exception of Class "E" (1913) and the 1920 "F" stock, all these cars had clerestory roofs, and ran in very mixed formations, though the "F" stock was not compatible with other types and so always ran in block trains. The Piccadilly Line, in addition to the extension to Uxbridge in October 1933, had also been opened to Cockfosters at the northern end, and so orders were placed for a large batch of new rolling stock, built in 1931-4, of "Standard" tube stock. This sufficed until 1952, when 15 trains of 1938 tube stock, with increased accommodation, were transferred to the Piccadilly Line. On December 14th 1959 the first lightweight stock, with unpainted aluminium panels, was placed in service.

This was followed by 1972 Mark 1 and Mark 2 stock, these also have unpainted aluminium panels and are broadly similar in design, but the Mark 2 stock had red-painted doors and the LT roundel on the bodysides whereas the Mark 1 stock carried the "London Transport" lettering. 1972 stock trains are still working the Piccadilly Line services today, usually in 7-car formations.

Some Competition –
Trams and Buses

Trams provided the first effective competition to the railways; very often they were able to offer lower fares and a multitude of stopping places more convenient to travellers' needs than the often widely-spaced stations. In the earliest days the great tramcars were not so impeded by other traffic as when motor buses and taxis and motor cars began to flood the highways.

In Middlesex the tramway system was owned by the County Council and leased to the Metropolitan Electric Tramways company. The electric tramway reached Wembley in 1908 and was extended to its final outer terminus at Sudbury in 1910. Although, of course, the management of M.E.T. enjoyed a great deal of operational freedom the County Council could insist on the provision of social facilities such as cheap-rate early morning workmens' cars, and exercised a right of control of fares charged. M.E.T. established a depot at Stonebridge Park on the main line of their route from Paddington to the "Swan" at Sudbury. On the OS map of 1914/5 Stonebridge Park tram depot and railway station are shown still set in a largely green environment – the "Coach and Horses'" pub,the Palace, Stonebridge Farm, a couple of recreation grounds and little else, although to the south east the various LNWR sidings of the Harlesden/Willesden area sparkled and interlocked like giant chain-mail.

By 1913 Service 62 Paddington-Sudbury was on a generally six minute interval basis. The coming of the Exhibition of 1924 spurred a great deal of activity on the tramways. Route 58 linked Paddington with Wembley Hill Road only (nearest point to the Exhibition grounds); a new route 68 ran from Acton to Sudbury. A new crossover was installed at Wembley Hill Road and on a number of routes provision was augmented. Special cars from distant parts of the network, often for school parties, carried boards such as 'Special Through Car For Wembley Exhibition' etc.

The London County Council commenced operations on Route 30 from Putney Church to Wembley, extended later to Sudbury to avoid the congestion of turning in Wembley, and extended at the other end to Tooting making it London's longest ever tram route. During the period of the Exhibition Underground Railways issued combined train/tram tickets allowing tram travel between Sudbury Town station and Wembley.

Following the final closure of the Exhibition in 1925 after its second year's opening, tram Route 68 was withdrawn and, over the years LCC Route 30 was truncated at various points, sometimes in relation to greyhound racing at Wembley. For a time in the thirties bus competition prompted the withdrawal of Sunday trams between Stonebridge Park depot and Sudbury. Cup Finals and other football matches produced considerable occasional extra traffic.

From the end of 1933 the former LCC tram route 30 was withdrawn north of Harlesden and replaced by Route 28 Wembley-Victoria. The LPTB programme of replacement of trams by trolleybuses meant that in 1935, the conversion of Stonebridge Park depot for trolleybuses was started, and from 23rd August 1936 the route through Wembley became 662 trolleybus Paddington to Sudbury. The M.E.T. and London General Omnibus Co had a pooling arrangement for receipts on routes where they ran in parallel, but when independent 'pirate' bus operators proliferated in the '20's they eroded the viability of the trams in a big way; through the Wembley area there were as many as eighteen 'pirate' companies running east to west routes at one stage.

The 'General" Company developed its north west London services fairly slowly. By 1912 the only route through Wembley was No 60, a Sundays only service from Tottenham Court Road to Wealdstone. A backbone service which has remained important over the years, despite numerous route changes at either end is No 18 and the LGOC had to compete with a number of operators, such as Pioneer, on this lucrative operation.. The 1924 Exhibition encouraged a plethora of 'pirate' inroads; it was easy to get route approvals – one single bus "Regent" had approval for 24 routes, four from Wembley Park ... to Stoke Newington, East Ham, Liverpool Street, and Liverpool Street via Victoria! By 1925, however, the authorities had regulated the weekday schedules on Wembley routes and the buccaneers had only Sundays on which to raid in the bigger fishes' preserves. An eight "platform" bus station was in use at the South East Entrance to the Exhibition capable of handling 20,000 passengers an hour. Even after a period of amalgamation and mass acquisitions London had 64 independent operators on 169 schedules.

Trolleybuses replaced trams and by the end of the Hitler War route 662, Paddington-Sudbury, had a service interval of 3-10 minutes and cars were timed to take 38 minutes for the complete journey.

With the partial de-regulation of London's buses in 1995 there is a plethora of operators providing the services deemed essential by London Transport – Armchair, Metro-line, London Buslines, Challenger and others – and in some cases providing additional routes on their own account. Brent Council subsidised temporarily one Sundays only service. A comprehensive Wembley area bus guide and map is published by London Transport Buses.

A curious time-table of Staff Travel facilities was published for a time for the Bakerloo line which included scheduled and numbered taxi provision; for example cab(s) left Elephant & Castle at 12 54 am calling at all stations except Charing Cross as far as North Wembley, thence diverting to Harrow on the Hill arriving at 1.45am.

At Sudbury terminus. Type "A" 8-wheel car No. 81 (later LPTB 2418).

APPENDIX 1 – PLAN OF WEST COAST MAIN LINE

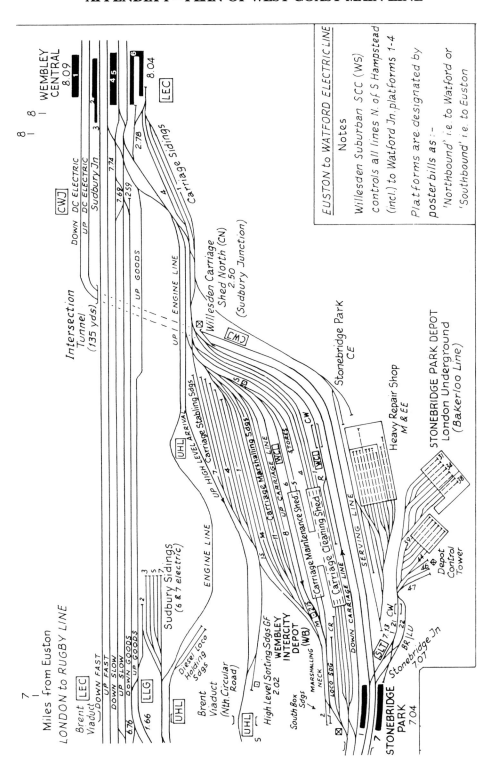

Wembley track layout 1990 – a section from the West Coast Main line in "London Midland Regional Track Diagrams" by kind permission of the publishers Quail Map Co., Exeter.

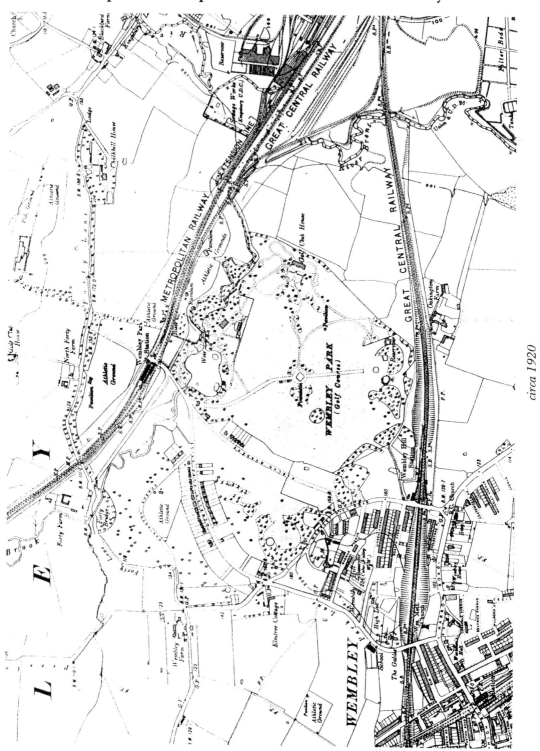

circa 1920

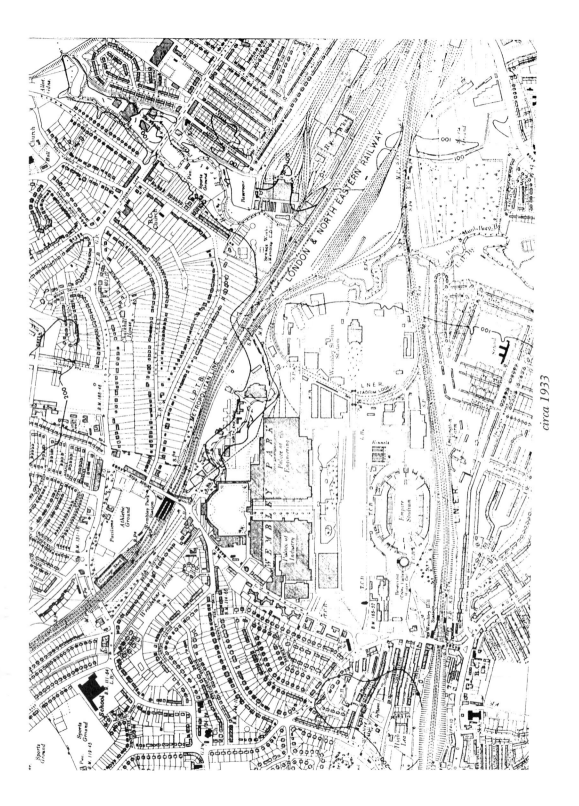

circa 1933

65

APPENDIX 3 – SPECIMEN TICKETS
(By kind permission of and with the generous assistance of the Transport Ticket Society)

LNWR - LMS - BRITISH RAILWAYS

BTC Edmondson, 14th January, 1957.

BRB Rapidprinter, circa 1970.

EXHIBITION NEVER-STOP RAILWAY

17th June, 1937.

29th January, 1940.

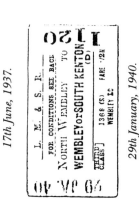

66

METROPOLITAN - MET. & GREAT CENTRAL - LONDON TRANSPORT

DISTRICT - LONDON TRANSPORT

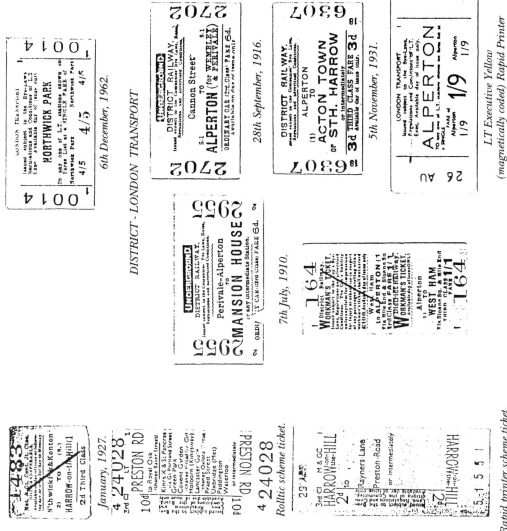

6th December, 1962.

28th September, 1916.

5th November, 1931.

LT Executive Yellow
(magnetically coded) Rapid Printer

7th July, 1910.

January, 1927.

Rolltic scheme ticket.

Rapid printer scheme ticket.

17th December, 1898.

24th October, 1921.

28th September, 1932 (new station)

18th December, 1932.

67

L. N. E. R.
DAY EXCURSION
F.A. Cup Final 27 APRIL 1935.
LINCOLN (T. S.) to
WEMBLEY (STADIUM STATION)
AND BACK
Via KING'S CROSS & MARYLEBONE
FOR CONDITIONS SEE BACK
THIRD / — 58? CLASS
WEMBLEY STAD. STN.

0651

L. N. E. R. (S.T. 1502)
DAY EXCURSION
17 MAY 1949
BRADFORD (EXCH.) to
WEMBLEY (STADIUM STN)
AND BACK
Via King's Cross & Marylebone
VALID AS PER BILLS
THIRD CLASS
FOR CONDITIONS SEE BACK

0396

Single   2nd
Wembley Complex
to
London (Marylebone)
HALF
Price 25p   (M)
For conditions see over

0843

5th November, 1931.

THE PRESENT STATION

Class	Ticket type	Adult	Child
STD	SGL SINGLE	ONE	NIL SGL

Date   Number
15-MAY-90   16678   4593150?W01
            Valid   Price
From   £1.40M
WEMBLEY STADIUM ON DATE SHOWN
LONDON BRIT RAIL   Route   2204

5th November, 1931.

L. N. E. R.
FOR CONDITIONS SEE BACK. Available for three days, including day of issue.
SUDBURY & HARROW ROAD to
SUDBURY HILL (HARROW)
Fare   S   2LC CLASS
THIRD   2183
            SUDBURY HILL H.

2820

14th December, 1957.

L. N. E. R.
FOR CONDITIONS SEE BACK. Available for three days including day of issue.
WEMBLEY HILL to
SUDBURY HILL (HARROW)
Third Class   Fare 9d.Z

0642

25th October, 1958.

L. N. E. R.
For conditions see back
Available on day of
issue only.
WEMBLEY S. Stn (12) WEMBLEY S. Stn (2)
WEMBLEY STADIUM STN (2) to
MARBLE ARCH BOND STREET or
TOTTENHAM COURT ROAD
MARBLE ARCH etc. MARBLE ARCH etc.
to Marylebone & Oxford Circus
3rd. 1s.—   3rd. 15.5+d.Z

0030

31st July, 1948.

L. & N. E. Ry.
NOT TRANSFERABLE
Issued subject to the Regulations and Conditions in the Company's Timetables, Books, Bills &c.
Day Excursion 28. APRIL 1923.
ON BATH OF ISSUE ONLY.
MARYLEBONE
TO
EXHIBITION Grounds Station
AND BACK
THIRD CLASS   Fare 1s.10d.

9937

28th April, 1923
(note the name prior to opening of exhibition.)

L. N. E. R.
APRIL 24. 1926.
WEMBLEY EXHIBITION STN to
MARYLEBONE
THIRD CLASS 10d.

0819

29th April, 1926.

L. N. E. R.
NOT TRANSFERABLE.
Issued subject to the Regulations and Conditions of the Company's Time Tables, Books, Bills & Notices
ON DATE OF ISSUE ONLY.
EXHIBITION STATION (2)
TO
MARYLEBONE
THIRD CLASS   Fare 10d
ADULT

9988

3rd June, 1924.

3rd-SINGLE   SINGLE—3rd
WEMBLEY STADIUM 1
to
Wembley Stad. 1   WembleyStad. 1
Marylebone   Marylebone
THIRD CLASS   ADULT
(W) 1/1   Fare 1/1 (W)
For conditions see over for conditions see over

6302

19th November, 1936.

68

APPENDIX 4
BRITISH TRANSPORT POLICE

There are few more memorable images of the British 'Bobby' as a patient, capable father-figure than the lone policeman on his grey horse coping with the pitch-invading thousands at the 1923 Cup Final.

George Scorey, the mounted policeman in question had, in fact, been on duty in Central London when ordered by Rochester Row Police Station to go and deal with a crowd problem at Wembley. Apparently, when he asked how he was to get there he was told: "Ride up the Edgware Road and turn left!"

Despite the huge crowds which attend major events at Wembley, until fairly recently railway crowd control was exercised by police designated 'Wembley Park officers' but based at and despatched from Baker Street as appropriate.

In 1989 a new British Transport Police station was opened just to the north of Wembley Park station, and its lines of responsibility currently are – Kilburn to Stanmore on the Jubilee, Wembley Park to all points outward on the Metropolitan.(Amersham, Watford, Uxbridge), and the Piccadilly from Alperton to where it meets the Met. at Rayners Lane. Bakerloo (trains only, not stations) are supervised from Wembley Park on the section Kilburn Park to Watford Junction.

British Transport police force at Wembley Park consists of an Inspector, 4 Sergeants, 26 Police Constables and 3 Detectives. Obviously, on important occasions these officers are reinforced from elsewhere. The present numbers of fans using the railways to reach Wembley on Cup Final days, for instance, are of the order of 40-45,000 homeward bound but a larger number of journeys are made prior to the match as many supporters arrive very early and make a trip to the metropolis before kick-off.

DOUGLAS STUCKEY

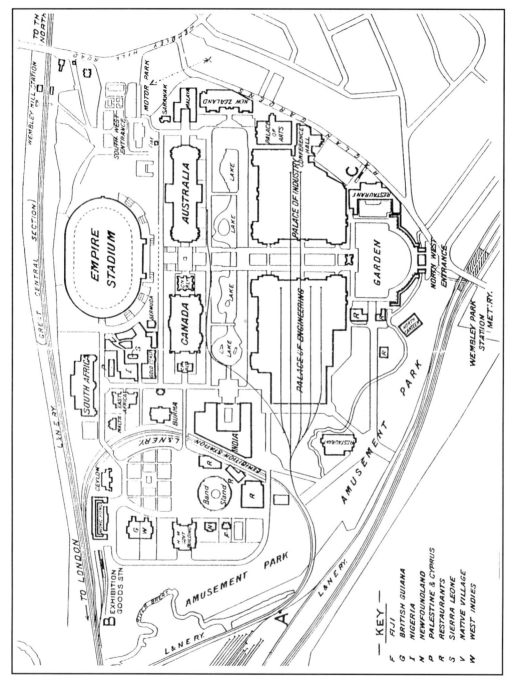

Plan of the Empire Exhibition site. The LNER loop line can be seen on the left with Wembley Park station at the bottom. Also shown are the sidings used to bring the railway and other heavy exhibits into the Palace of Engineering.

70

Some Sources
of Information

The Age of the Electric Train by J. C. Gillham (Ian Allan, 1988).

British Rail Track Diagrams (London, Midland & Scottish Region)(Quail Map Co, 1990).

District Railway Board Minutes and other papers

The Final Link by Dennis Edwards and Ron Pigram (Midas Book, 1982).

The Great Central Railway, Volumes 2 & 3, by George Dow (Ian Allan, 1965).

Great Central Railway and LNER Board Minutes and other papers (Public Record Office).

Great Eastern Album by R. C. Riley (Ian Allan, 1968).

The History of the London & North Western Railway by Wilfred L. Steel (The Railway and Travel Monthly, 1914).

A History of Wembley (Brent Library Service, 1979)

London's Metropolitan Railway by Alan A. Jackson (David & Charles, 1986).

London & North Western Electrics by F. G. B. Atkinson and B.W. Adams (Electric Railway Society).

The London & North Western Railway by O. S. Nock (Ian Allan, 1960).

London Transport Rolling Stock & Locomotives (Ian Allan Ltd., 1978)

The Making of Modern London by David Wightman and Steve Humphreys (Sidgwick & Jackson, 1984).

Metro-Land 1927 editon (Metropolitan Railway).

Metropolitan Railway Board Minute Books and General Manager's Papers.

Metropolitan Railway Electric Locomotives by K. R. Benest (Lens of Sutton, 1963).

Metropolitan Railway Rolling Stock and Train Services (article by G. T. Moody in the *Railway Observer,* January 1935).

The Metropolitan Today (article by B. Perren in *Trains Illustrated,* November 1955).

Metropolitan Tower Construction Company Minutes.

Notes on petrol-electric railcar by Robert Barker.

A Short History of Road-Rails and Never-Stop Railway Systems (Wembley Transport Society).

Metropolitan Electric Tramways (Volumes 1 & 2) by C. S. Smeeton (Light Railway Transit Assoc., 1984 and 1986 respectively.

S.L.S. Journal, May 1976 (article on locomotives lent to Neasden G.C. Engine shed).

Sudbury Hill, Harrow, article by R. M. S. Hall, Steam Days, July/September, 1989.

The Welsh Harp, article by Clifford Morsley in Country Life, 15th July, 1965.

Wembley Park Estate Company Minutes.

ACKNOWLEDGEMENTS

The Author and Publishers wish to thank sincerely the people and organisations who have helped us with this book.

Unfortunately, it is impossible to name them all individually but they include: The General Electric Co., Greater London Record Office, InterCity West Coast, Libraries of Brent and Harrow, Oliver Green and the London Transport Museum, Brian Morrison, North London Railways, Railfreight Distribution, John Shelbourn of the Transport Ticket Society and Wembley Stadium.

Wembley Central station is leased by North London Railways from Railtrack and they are responsible for the day-to-day management of the station which is also used by Bakerloo trains.

As we write 2nd June 1996, is expected to see a new off-peak 30 minute interval service, bringing into use the up and down slow lines for the first time for many years. These trains will also serve Watford Junction, Bushey, Harrow and Wealdstone and Euston, and later may stop at the slow line platforms at Willesden Junction which is being developed as a 'hub' station allowing greatly improved interchange between the various routes. Major sporting or other events at Wembley require extensive planning and co-ordination between the various railway operators, police and other parties. Euro 96 (European Football Championships) bringing vast numbers of supporters from the continent took 15 months planning to ensure all arrangements meet the stringent criteria imposed. Communication links were established between the three Wembley stations (Central/Stadium/Park) using the London Underground mobile communications organisation to secure trouble-free and co-ordinated transport facilities.

From information supplied by Mr Dennis Lovett, External Liaison Manager, North London Railways.

"Rus in Urbe" – Award-winning garden beds at Preston Road looking north, Autumn 1995.

DOUGLAS STUCKEY

Inside cover exhibition pictures are with permission from Len Snow's *"Pictorial History of Brent"* (Phillimore).